Richard Deming traces civil law from its origins in primitive societies through contemporary civil processes. He discusses the various circumstances over which civil courts preside, examining such actions as compensation for wrongs, legislation for rectifying wrongs, payment of debts, and procedures to enforce money judgments. He also covers actions of equity, including custody actions, divorce and bankruptcy. A large section of the book is devoted to suits for personal injury, which account for 80 percent of all civil actions. And lastly, the author takes a critical look at court procedures and proposes valuable reforms that could lead to a more effective system.

RICHARD DEMING has been a lay student of the law for some twenty years. Over that period he has conducted extensive research for background material for the numerous crime and mystery novels he has written. He has made thorough studies of four major city police departments and has been a dedicated observer of municipal and state courtroom procedures all over the country.

Man Against Man

CIVIL LAW AT WORK

Richard Deming

WILDSIDE PRESS

For Barbara

CONTENTS

PREFACE

This is the second book in a series of three whose purpose is to explain, in lay terms, how our legal system functions. The first was titled *Man and Society: Criminal Law at Work*. This one concerns civil law. The third and last of the series will cover international law. Except for some historical material on the origins and development of criminal law, the first book concerned itself primarily with criminal law in the United States. In this book also some historic material has been given in order to show how civil law developed, but again the story of how the law functions has been confined essentially to how it functions in our own country.

This is neither a how-to-save-money-by-being-your-own-lawyer book nor a legal-pitfalls-to-avoid book. Enough of each type already abound. This book is solely intended to explain, in as clear and as interesting terms as I have been able to devise, how civil law works in the United States.

The term *civil law* has two quite separate meanings, only one of which concerns us. The usage with which we are *not* concerned is when the term denotes the type of legal system a particular country has. Those countries that have codified systems of law, such as France's Code Napoléon, are said to be *civil-law* countries, as opposed to *common-law* countries such as

England and the United States. (The term *common law* has two different meanings also. As used in this series, unless otherwise stated, it means custom or usage so widespread that it is recognized as having the force of law. As used as an antonym to civil law in the latter's above sense, it means a system of law in general force throughout an entire nation or a specific portion of a nation, such as one of our United States, which is based not only on statute but also upon custom and precedent. In civil-law countries law is created only by legislative act or decree, and judicial decisions can neither change the law nor be cited as precedents in subsequent cases. In common-law countries judicial decisions become part of the law and carry as much weight as statutes. In fact in a sense they carry more weight, in that judicial decisions can overturn legislative acts.)

Civil law in the sense that we are concerned with is the law governing the personal relations between individuals, as distinguished from criminal law, which concerns the relations between individuals and the state. Civil law is sometimes referred to as *private law,* as distinguished from *public law.* Public law, which includes criminal law, is so called because it is deemed to be of importance to the public at large. Private law is deemed to be of concern only to the litigants, although a civil case can sometimes have a profound effect upon the entire community (a citizen's suit to halt the building of an industrial plant on the grounds that it may pollute the environment, for example). As will be seen when we get into such matters as *torts,* or civil wrongs, there is some overlapping of civil and criminal law. For the most part, however, the two fields are clearly enough separated to justify their study as separate subjects.

As was mentioned in the preface to the first book, no one has ever succeeded in adequately defining the word *law,* despite history's greatest legal minds bending their talents to the task. As a random example, the famous English jurist Sir William Blackstone, one of the great legal minds of all time, defined "a law" as "a rule of civil conduct prescribed by the supreme power in a state, commanding what is right and prohibiting what is wrong." This seems like a nice, clear definition until you try defining "right" and "wrong."

It is not a great deal easier to define the three subdivisions of law into which this trilogy is divided; however, some sort of definitions are necessary simply to distinguish between the three. In the preface to *Man and Society* I gave the definition of "criminal law" as "that branch of the law which defines crimes and fixes penalties for them," then further defined "a crime" as "a voluntary violation of a law enacted to invoke the responsibility of individuals to the community, and therefore an act injurious to the public. It may be either an act of commission or omission. That is, it may be a positive act, such as theft, or a negative act, such as failure to file an income-tax return."

Although this definition is far from perfect, it is a reasonable description of criminal law. For this study I will attempt to define "civil law." The definition of "international law" can wait for the final book.

"Civil law" may be defined as that branch of the law which regulates the legal responsibilities of persons to each other in their private capacities and resolves disputes between them. The term "persons" in this definition includes not only individuals but also partnerships, corporations, nonprofit organizations of all types, the various levels of government, the branches of such levels of government, or any other entity capable of bringing or defending a court action.

In *Man and Society* we examined in some detail the court systems of three representative states: California, New York, and Missouri. In order to retain some degree of uniformity, we will emphasize those same three states in this study, although we will not confine ourselves exclusively to them. This will involve looking at some of the same courts we studied in the previous book, but in that we considered only their criminal-law functions, and this time we will be considering only their civil-law functions.

I wish to extend my thanks to attorney Edwin L. Laing, of Ventura, California, for checking the script for legal errors. He should not be held accountable for any of the opinions expressed, as his help was limited to pointing out inaccuracies. All opinions expressed are strictly those of the author.

R. D.

Man Against Man

Chapter **1**

THE ORIGINS OF CIVIL LAW
AND OF THE LEGAL PROFESSION

As with criminal law, most of what we know about civil law in primitive societies is based on anthropological studies of present-day primitive tribes. We know nothing about the legal procedures of Stone Age man for the simple reason that he kept no historical records. Since certain basic procedures are common to the civil law of most modern primitive societies, however, it is reasonable to assume that our remote cavemen ancestors practiced similar procedures.

In primitive societies civil law was concerned almost solely with reparation for wrongs. The purely regulatory matters that make up so large a part of modern civil law, such as marriage, divorce, and adoption, were concerns of either religion or custom rather than of the law. Initially the primary function of civil law was merely to redress the wrongs perpetrated on tribe members by other members of the same tribe. Civil wrongs, both in Stone Age times and today, are of two types: wrongs against persons and wrongs against property.

In primitive societies there was generally no recognition of real property rights. *Real property* is land and things attached to the land, such as buildings or other structures, as opposed to *personal property,* which includes all other types of possessions. Your home is real property; your car is personal property.

It is almost certain that our cavemen ancestors held no recognized legal rights to the caves they lived in, other than the right of possession. When one occupant moved out, anyone else who chose to could move in without requiring any permission from the previous occupant. Nor could any individual claim possession of a section of land or a spring or a stream.

The concept of personal property goes back into the dim reaches of time, however. Probably the moment some ancient savage ancestor of ours first picked up a stick to use as a weapon or as a tool to knock down a piece of fruit beyond the reach of his bare hands, the concept was born. A mere claim of ownership is quite different from recognition of the right of ownership, though, and initially there was probably no widespread acceptance of such a right. Stronger tribe members instead probably regarded it as *their* right to appropriate for themselves any items that appealed to them that were in the possession of weaker members.

Very early in time the exclusive right to personal property such as weapons and tools must have been recognized by the tribe, though, and custom probably fixed simple forms of compensation for violations of such rights. If Bearclaw borrowed Deerfoot's stone ax, for instance, and accidentally broke the handle, he was bound by custom to refit it with a new handle. He didn't do this simply because he felt a moral obligation or through fear of Deerfoot's anger—although he might feel both—but because custom decreed that Deerfoot had the right to get back his property in the same condition that he had loaned it.

Among many modern primitive tribes there is also the concept of the right of exclusive use of certain real property, even when there is no recognition of the ownership of real property. The man who discovers a particularly heavy-bearing fruit tree in the jungle, for instance, may place an individual mark upon it, reserving it for his exclusive use. He is not claiming ownership but only his right, by virtue of discovery, to harvest the tree's fruit.

It is quite probable that this concept also developed among some of our Stone Age ancestors, and again the right must have eventually come to be accepted by all other members of the tribe. If the right was violated, compensation was due the tree's discoverer, but in this case compensation was not quite as simple as in the case of the broken ax handle, since the stolen fruit could hardly be replaced on the tree. Something of equivalent value had to be given to the wronged party: perhaps another type of food, such as fish, perhaps a spear or a knife. Initially the proper compensation in such cases must have been either mutually agreed upon in each instance or decreed by the tribe's elders, but eventually custom fixed exact forms of compensation for specific wrongs.

Incidentally, in modern primitive societies the concept of exclusive use never extends to natural facilities necessary to the general welfare of the tribe. No one, by right of discovery, can claim exclusive use of a spring or of the fishing rights to a stream, although in the latter case he might be permitted to mark a particular fishing spot as his own. Even his right to harvest the fruit of a particular tree would probably be limited if it were the *only* such tree available.

From these primitive beginnings of a system to adjust noncriminal wrongs there gradually developed the institution of *composition*. This was the custom of compensating a wronged individual in some specific way that tradition had come to consider the proper compensation for the particular wrong involved. It might have been simply to give a feast for the wronged one in public atonement, or it might have been the presentation of gifts of specific value. In either case the composition was set by fixed custom.

Anthropologists are generally agreed that compositions were probably originally paid as peace terms following physical retaliation against the person committing the wrong. Since blood feuds were common among primitive tribes, such retaliation often involved not just the wronged person attacking the one who wronged him but his whole family attacking the kin of the offender. The feud would end only when a satisfactory composition was paid to the person wronged.

Inevitably there came a time in the development of all primitive societies when the institution of composition flourished; blood feuds disappeared, because tradition had come to fix such specific compositions that they were deemed to be all the satisfaction necessary. A remarkable thing about the custom is that it developed in a very high form among a number of primitive tribes that had no court systems of any sort. Among these were the Yurok, an Indian stock of northwestern California, who fixed an exact composition for every injury to a person or his property. The Ifugao, a Philippine tribe of Malay origin which once practiced headhunting, had a detailed scale that fixed median compositions for every type of injury, then adjusted them upward or downward according to the social rank of the wronged person. In both groups compositions were religiously paid according to custom without any enforcement procedure other than public opinion.

Various criteria were used in fixing the amounts of composition in different tribes, but usually these amounts had some practical basis rather than merely being arbitrarily fixed by chiefs, priests, or tribal councils. For instance, the common composition paid a father for the abduction of a daughter in most modern primitive tribes where the system is in effect is the bride price he would have asked of a suitor who wooed her in a more orthodox manner. Similarly the composition for accidentally causing the death of a child is often the bride price that was paid for the victim's mother.

Deliberate homicide in primitive tribes was seldom compensable by composition. Although there are instances of primitive tribes wherein murder was regarded as a civil wrong against the victim's kin instead of a crime, they are rare. Many tribes considered murder a personal matter between the murderer and the victim's relatives rather than as the business of the tribe, but it was still regarded as a crime. Acceptance of composition for it was generally looked down upon as taking "blood money." Avenging the death with blood was regarded as the only honorable retaliation.

Since composition payments were usually in the form of livestock, vegetables, and grain, the institution flourished mainly in agricultural tribes. It remained an equitable method of compensating for civil wrongs only so long as life remained fairly simple, however. It was fine for primitive tribes. It was unworkable in more complex societies.

The reason for this is that in primitive societies there were seldom any vast differences in wealth. A tribal chief might have owned fifty cows, whereas the poorest member of the tribe owned only two, but the economic gulf between them was not tremendous. It was nothing compared to the gulf between aristocrats and peasants during the Middle Ages or, to give a more

modern example, compared to the gulf between How-
ard Hughes and the average factory worker. Even to
the chief of a primitive tribe the payment of a cow as
composition was a substantial economic loss. As society became more complex, however, wealth inevitably became concentrated in fewer and fewer hands.
Eventually the point was reached where composition
was no deterrent to the abuse of rights of the poor by
the rich, because the latter could make legal redress
for their abuses merely by tossing the victims or their
survivors a few coins. The institution of composition
had firmly established the principle that even unintentional wrongs should be compensated, but the accompanying principle that each type of wrong had a
fixed price had outlived its usefulness by the time
civilization began to develop.

It is interesting to note that compositions were payable only to men. Women, being property themselves,
had no property rights. Even in the event of a composition paid for the death of a husband, it was payable
not to the widow but to the male relative who had
assumed responsibility for her support. Such responsibility was fixed by custom. Usually the eldest son
assumed it. If there were no sons, the dead man's
brothers were usually next in line, then various other
relatives of the dead man. The widow's blood relatives
assumed responsibility only if there was no one left in
her husband's family, because having been sold to her
husband, she was the responsibility of his family, not
hers.

This progression of responsibility obtained even in
the so-called matriarchal societies. Modern anthropologists have come to the nearly unanimous conclu-
sion that primitive societies dominated by women are

wholly mythical. The legendary Amazons never really existed except in storytellers' imaginations. All that most so-called matriarchates amounted to was that descent was traced through the female line and a mother's children belonged to her clan instead of to their father's. There is no evidence that women held ruling authority in any society, ever. Their dominance, if any, was largely ritualistic. In ancient China, for instance, even a grown son was expected to prostrate himself before his mother and beg forgiveness if he offended her, yet she had no property rights and might be totally dependent on the son for her support.

Like the Yurok and the Ifugao, the earliest ancestors of Western man probably had no court system. Since compositions were rigidly fixed by custom, it was unnecessary to have judges to decree the amounts of damages to be paid, nor were courts necessary for enforcement, because public opinion took care of that. Any defendant who defied tradition by refusing to pay composition could expect social ostracism, which in primitive societies was a far more fearsome punishment than anything modern judges hand down for contempt of court.

Although compositions were fixed, there were inevitable disagreements between those who claimed to have been wronged and those they accused—today we would call them plaintiffs and defendants—as to whether or not a wrong had actually been done. Among the most primitive tribes such disagreements generally could be worked out to the satisfaction of both parties merely by discussion. Since primitive men are usually remarkably truthful, even in confessing misdeeds, an innocent defendant could usually expect his accuser to accept his plea of innocence, but as mankind moved from a state of savagery into the more advanced state of barbarism,* men began to lose their childlike faith in fellowmen. Plaintiffs no longer were willing to accept the unsupported word of defendants but began to demand proof of innocence. In cases where the offered evidence still failed to satisfy the plaintiffs, they began to demand judgment by an impartial referee.

Initially no special offices were created to decide such matters, the referees simply being members of the existing tribal apparatus. In some cases the tribal chief acted as judge; in other cases it was a priest; in still others the entire tribal council would hear the arguments of both sides. In the beginning it is probable that the person or group chosen to hand down a decision was mutually agreed upon by both parties, but custom must have quickly caused certain persons in each tribe to be singled out as judges. Once this began to happen, litigants lost the right of mutually agreeing on who should decide their differences and thereafter had to submit them to the judges designated by the tribe. The earliest actual records of litigations suggest that they were before such established tribunals instead of before mutually agreed-upon judges. From what scanty records there are of liti-

---

*The anthropological definition of the "savage" state is one in which living conditions are little above those of animals, the only government is a tribal chieftain whose only two functions are to lead the tribe in battle and on the hunt, and the only law consists of religious taboos. Stone Age man is classified as a savage. The intermediate stage between savagery and civilization is called barbarism. Although a more highly developed society than savagery, the barbaric stage still keeps no historic records and has no written laws, but it does have a legal system based on custom. Often there is no written language, and when there is one, it seldom consists of more than a simple system of symbols.

gations among the barbaric tribes of Europe—mainly accounts in sagas and poems—the burden of proof rested on the defendant, and neither the litigants nor witnesses were sworn. Decisions handed down by tribal courts were final, as there were no higher courts to which to appeal.

During the barbaric period *trial by ordeal* first began to appear. (This was virtually unknown among savage tribes.) Under this system the truth was determined by submitting the defendant to some physical test. Among the more unreasonable tests were *trial by fire* and *trial by water*. In the former the defendant would be required to thrust his hand into a fire or perhaps to pick up a glowing coal. If he was burned, he was deemed to be lying; if unscathed, he was telling the truth. Trial by water involved being immersed for a period of time—perhaps five minutes. If the witness drowned, his testimony was false; if he survived, it was true.

Actually historians have exaggerated the prevalence of trial by ordeal in Europe, particularly in civil suits. The more violent ordeals, such as trial by fire and trial by water, were used only in criminal cases, and even then they were never widespread. Although for a time during the Middle Ages they became rather standard procedure in witchcraft and sorcery cases, trial by ordeal was rare in other criminal cases, even for capital offenses, and it was usually employed in civil cases only as a last resort, when judges were unable to form opinions based solely on the evidence.

In such cases the ordeal was usually far less drastic than those used in criminal trials. A common test was to blindfold the defendant and require him to touch one of two objects, usually either a dagger or a cross. If he chose the dagger, he lost the case; if he chose the cross, he won. Although hardly the soundest way in judicial history to decide a lawsuit, at least it was no more unfair to one litigant than to the other. What it amounted to was both sides agreeing to abide by the flip of a coin.

Trial by ordeal lasted through the Middle Ages, although it began to fall into disuse after 1215, when the Fourth Lateran Council forbade the clergy to participate in such tests. The system persisted in some secular courts to the end of the seventeenth century, though. It was even imported by early colonists to America (where it was unknown to the original Indian inhabitants) and was employed in witchcraft trials as late as 1698.

Somewhat similar to trial by ordeal was the institution of *trial by battle.* This was a common practice among savage tribes but for some odd reason seems to have been unknown among the barbaric tribes of Europe ("odd" because it was common among some American Indian tribes, and anthropologists classify American Indians of pre-Colonial days as barbarians rather than as savages). Since litigation had developed largely to end the blood feud as a means of settling disputes between members of the same tribe, perhaps the explanation is that trial by battle fell into the same sort of disfavor. We can assume that it disappeared during barbaric times because verbal duels before a tribunal had simply taken the place of duels with weapons, but during the legal chaos of the Middle Ages it was often hard to find a court of competent jurisdiction in civil matters. Thus trial by battle was revived from prehistoric times during the era of feudalism.

Under the feudal system in Europe each baron decreed the law for the territory he controlled and established his own courts to administer it. The resulting hodgepodge of courts drove a good deal of litigation into the ecclesiastical courts, where more uniform rules applied. This was all right for common citizens, who usually took their disputes before these church courts by mutual agreement because both sides felt they were more likely to get justice there than in the baronial courts, but when knights were involved in legal disputes, particularly if they served under different barons, it was obviously to the advantage of each disputant to have the case tried before a court of his own baron.

Since it was seldom possible to get a knight defendant to agree to a trial before a court of the plaintiff's baron, and a plaintiff was equally reluctant to press a claim before a court of the defendant's baron, what it amounted to was that it was virtually impossible to bring civil suit in such cases. The result was that it became the custom to settle such disputes on the jousting field. The winner of the battle also won his case. Knightly honor upheld the decision. It was unheard of for a defeated plaintiff to further pursue his claim or for a defeated defendant to refuse to pay the claim demanded.

Trial by battle disappeared on the Continent with the death of feudalism, but rather incredibly it lingered on in England until the nineteenth century. In 1818 the plaintiff in a case known in English legal annals as *Ashford v. Thornton* challenged the defendant to trial by battle and won his case by winning the duel. The presiding judge held that trial by battle was recognized under English common law, even though it had not been invoked by anyone for many years. Parliament took care of that the next year. In 1819, as a direct result of *Ashford v. Thornton,* it passed an act abolishing trial by battle as a legal procedure.

Once litigants began to submit their legal disputes to disinterested referees for settlement, it was only a matter of time before trials became more and more formalized. Probably a number of factors contributed to this increasing formalization, but two probably contributed most heavily. The first was simply the human desire for guidelines to follow when confronted with unfamiliar situations. The following story illustrates what I mean by this.

One of the commonest complaints from Peace Corps field workers was that their work was hampered by the mass of rules and regulations issued from Washington which they were required to follow. When a study was undertaken to see if procedures could be simplified, it was discovered that the first Peace Corps workers had been sent out to underdeveloped areas all over the world with virtually no specific instructions other than the vague directive to "do good." Almost immediately they had begun to besiege Washington with requests for instructions on how to do everything from requisition material to convince tribal chieftains that garbage should be buried instead of being thrown in the village streets. It quickly became clear that most of the huge number of directives field workers were complaining hampered their efforts with red tape had originally been inspired by requests from earlier field workers for specific guidelines. Similarly, much of the initial formalization of trial procedures probably stemmed simply from this quite human desire for guidance along unfamiliar routes.

The second factor was the appointment of permanent judges by the political rulers to dispense justice in the names of the rulers. These judges, like all bureaucrats, had a vested interest in red tape. The favorite method of bureaucrats to perpetuate themselves in office is to establish a set of complicated rules for the general public to contend with in dealing with them, then to make themselves indispensable by becoming experts on the rules. In order to entrench themselves as the official dispensers of justice, the judges established increasingly rigid procedures that had to be followed. This began quite early, while most of Europe was still in the barbaric state, even before the rise of Greek and Roman civilizations.

Among the Germanic barbarians procedures became so rigid that if a plaintiff failed to observe some simple formality, he could lose his case then and there. An ancient German ballad tells of a plaintiff who haled a defendant into court because the latter had killed his bull. Because the plaintiff referred to the animal as a "bull" instead of by the legally acceptable term of "leader of the herd," the plaintiff lost his case. Even during the Roman Empire procedure sometimes held sway over justice. Gaius, one of Rome's greatest law teachers, who lived in the second century B.C., wrote of a litigant who lost a claim for damages to his vineyard because he referred to the damaged plants as "vines" when they were legally classified as "trees."

As court procedure became more complicated, it naturally became less wise for litigants to attempt to plead their own cases. The inevitable result was the emergence of a class of specialists who had memorized all the rules and were willing to represent clients in court for a fee. Thus lawyers came into being.

There were no lawyers in savage or barbarian societies, nor even in early civilizations. In ancient Egypt, Babylonia, early ancient Greece, and early republican Rome litigants were required to plead their own cases unless unable to appear in court because of illness. In such instances relatives or friends could appear for them, but these representatives were regarded as proxies of the ill litigants rather than as their agents. Lawyers were unknown in the ancient civilizations of the Orient, too, such as China and India.

In the latter days of ancient Greece it eventually became a common practice to pretend illness when you were haled into court; then you were able to obtain representation by noted orators who could presumably sway the court in your favor more effectively than you could personally. Thus there arose a sort of semiprofessional class that performed something of the function of modern lawyers. These men did not restrict their oratory to the courtroom, however, but were available as speech-makers for any occasion. Nor were they necessarily versed in the law; they were more likely merely to be trained in logic. Moreover, in Athens at least, it was illegal for a litigant to have the same orator speak for him in more than one case, which precluded the possibility of building up much of a legal practice.

Similarly, in the middle years of the Roman Republic, around 350 B.C., it began to become common for litigants to be represented by advocates who pleaded their cases for them in the forum. Again these were not professional lawyers, but neither were they professional speech-makers. Usually they were wealthy patricians, often members of the Senate, who undertook to represent clients not for fees but merely for the glory of exhibiting their forensic skills. As often as not their prime motive was to draw a popular following so that they could obtain political advancement. After Rome became an empire, this tradition persisted. Among those who pleaded cases before Roman tribunals were some of the great names in Roman history: Cicero, Cato, Julius Caesar, Pompey, and others.

After the fall of the Roman Empire, advocacy disappeared. The Germanic barbarians who inherited the empire had no lawyers. In the early days of feudalism it was possible to have a friend or relative represent you in court, but there were no professional lawyers who made their livings from the practice of law, nor was the practice of legal representation encouraged. In most European courts it required special permission from the ruling baron to be represented by an attorney instead of pleading your own case. In England it was necessary to obtain a royal writ.

By the twelfth century, however, these restrictions had been largely relaxed, and representation in court by legal counsel began to be common. Most advocates were either parish priests or monks, but this was more the result of the educational system of the time (or rather the lack of it) than of any widespread interest in law among the clergy. For all except those who could afford private tutors, virtually the only way to learn to read and write was to enter either the secular priesthood or a monastery.

Monasticism is not unique to Christianity. It preceded Christ in many religions, notably among the Hindus, ancient Greeks, and Jews. In all religions, including Christianity, it differs from the priesthood in that the priest ministers to the religious needs of worshipers by conducting services and administering sacraments, whereas the monk—or religious, as he is also known—withdraws from the world in order to attain spiritual perfection through contemplation (although the monk may also be an ordained priest). Thus the monk ordinarily has little contact with anyone other than fellow monks. During the Middle Ages, though, so many men entered monasteries for motives other

than the attainment of spiritual perfection that contemplation became a secondary activity. Because
monasteries were the only repositories of learning
available to the average man, the commonest motive
was to get an education. As a result monks became
the teachers of the world, and the monasteries the only schools. Even the secular priests obtained their ed-
ucations from the monks.

In the Middle Ages they could be seen everywhere
and except for their dress, often lived lives little different from anyone else. On the whole they were not
particularly noted for their piety. In *The Canterbury Tales* Chaucer describes some very earthy
monks, and of course everyone is familiar with the
jovial Friar Tuck of Robin Hood's band of merry men.

Toward the end of the Middle Ages a class of lay
lawyers began to emerge. Craft guilds had become
widespread all over Europe and England by then, so
it was quite natural that eventually these lay lawyers
would form their own guilds. These ancestors of our
modern bar associations exerted political pressure to
bar the clergy from competing with them, with the result that in France and England laws were passed prohibiting clergymen from assisting in lawsuits in the
secular courts. (The lawmakers had no authority over
the ecclesiastical courts, of course.) Some legal historians believe that the origin of the advocate's wig in
English courts was an attempt by clergymen to get
around the law by concealing their shaven heads.

Since its beginnings in the twelfth century the legal
profession in the Western world has fluctuated considerably in prestige. By the fourteenth century, advocates in both Germany and France had become a
lesser order of nobility, on a social level with knights.
Yet in 1780 Frederick the Great, of Prussia, at-

tempted to abolish the bar entirely, and in 1790 the National Assembly of France attempted the same thing. Both attempts failed.

Possibly because the average person's first contact with the legal profession was a threat of lawsuit by some lawyer, the general attitude toward lawyers was one of mistrust. Sir Thomas More's *Utopia,* published in 1516, made the absence of lawyers a condition of the ideal state. The legislatures of a number of the original thirteen colonies in America showed similar hostility toward the legal profession. Georgia classed lawyers and rum as equivalent evils by barring the practice of the former and the sale of the latter in the same law. Virginia more subtly undermined the profession by allowing the practice of law but forbidding the charging of legal fees. Nevertheless the growth of shipping and trade in the colonies had developed a rich merchant class by the early 1700's which simply could not get along without legal advice. By the time of the American Revolution the practice of law was not only legal in all colonies but had also come to be accepted as an honorable profession.

From the time the legal profession first began to emerge as an influential force during the twelfth century, judges recognized in it a powerful potential ally in their effort to entrench themselves in power. (Today, of course, most judges are chosen from the legal profession, but when the lawyer guilds first began to form, the judiciary and the bar were quite separate professions.) Like the judges, lawyers had a vested interest in complicating court procedure. It brought them profit by making them essential. When written pleas began to replace oral arguments, clients found their help even more essential.

In all fairness it must be conceded that the system

of advocacy in itself played a large part in complicating court procedure. Unfortunately the system of pitting opposing attorneys against each other provides a built-in incentive to take advantage of legal technicalities and to use delaying tactics when such actions are deemed by lawyers to be in the best interests of their clients. So even the most highly motivated lawyers tended, by their legal maneuvering on behalf of clients, to complicate procedures. Also in all fairness it should be noted that anthropologists generally credit priests rather than lawyers with the first use of written pleas and written evidence, but lawyers quickly realized the larger profit that could be made from drawing up documents instead of merely entering oral pleas. Judges obligingly helped their lawyer allies and at the same time further entrenched themselves by eventually not only accepting written pleas in lieu of oral ones but also demanding them.

This development was particularly visible in England. Under the Anglo-Saxons litigation was entirely oral, and procedures had at least a minimum of flexibility. After the arrival of William the Conqueror, however, procedures become more rigid, and the use of written pleas steadily increased. By the sixteenth century a highly formal and complex system of civil law had developed.

In a typical suit for damages a plaintiff would file a *declaration,* which was simply a document outlining his claim against the defendant. The defendant would then file a *plea* denying the claim. The plaintiff could then file a *replication* disputing the plea, which the defendant might answer with a *rejoinder*. The plaintiff could counter this with a *rebutter,* which the defendant might answer with a *surrebutter*. All these documents were filed before the case actually got to the point of argument before a judge or jury, and if any one of them failed to follow the precise legal terminology required, the case could be lost then and there.

English courts have long since ceased to be quite so hidebound. There, and in all other countries with advanced legal systems, it is still necessary to file legal documents in connection with all but the most simple legal actions, but in both the so-called civil-law countries and the common-law countries a great many common-sense reforms have been made. In the United States, for instance, although documents submitted to the courts still must be in rather standard forms, and it is still possible for a pleading error to lose a case, it is not likely for a case to be lost simply because a lawyer strayed from the accepted terminology. If the terminology is clear to the court, often the document will be accepted without prejudice even if the "whereases" are in the wrong places. If it isn't clear, sometimes the judge will simply return it to the submitting lawyer for rewording. It should be understood, however, that this is a matter of judicial decision, and the judge *may* rule against the side guilty of the submitted error. It therefore behooves lawyers to do their homework instead of trusting to judicial leniency.

Although throughout legal history court procedures grew increasingly complicated, the modern trend is in the opposite direction. At least in American courts there has been a definite tendency ever since World War II to simplify procedure instead of further complicating it. As a prime example, only a few years ago appeals courts in most states refused to review adverse rulings made by trial judges unless the attorney for the side ruled against took a formal objection to the ruling. Here is an excerpt from a 1930 court record of a child-custody suit in St. Louis, Missouri, in which a divorced husband was attempting to get the custody of his six-year-old son from the mother. In this segment the ex-husband's lawyer is designated as "plaintiff," the ex-wife, who is on the stand, as "witness," and her lawyer as "defense."

PLAINTIFF: How would you class your drinking habits, Mrs. Slater? Would you say you are a heavy drinker, a temperate drinker, or a teetotaler?

WITNESS: Temperate.

PLAINTIFF: Wasn't the original separation between you and your husband, and the subsequent divorce, caused by arguments about your heavy drinking?

DEFENSE: Object as incompetent, irrelevant, and immaterial. The divorce between plaintiff and defendant is over and done with, and its causes have no bearing on this case. The only pertinent question is my client's competence as a mother *now*. She has answered counsel's question about her drinking habits as of this moment. What they were at some distant point in the past is irrelevant and immaterial.

COURT: Sustained. Counsel will confine himself to exploring the defendant's present qualifications as a parent.

PLAINTIFF: Exception.

This case, won by the defendant, was reversed by the Missouri court of appeal, which ordered a new trial on the grounds that the defendant's past drinking habits constituted pertinent evidence. At the second trial the husband was granted custody. At that time, however, if the plaintiff's lawyer had not uttered the single word "exception," the court of appeal would have refused to examine that portion of the trial record.

California and New York State were the first to abolish the rule that only those portions of trial records excepted to were subject to review, on the grounds that it was unfair to the litigant to deny him the relief of judicial review simply because his lawyer failed to shout "Exception!" at the proper time. Other states, including Missouri, have since followed, and it is probable that eventually the exception will be a thing of the past in all states.

In the above trial record there is another phrase that has also become almost a thing of the past. That is the defense objection as "incompetent, irrelevant, and immaterial." This phrase, once accompanying nearly every courtroom objection, has fallen into disuse because it is largely meaningless. The word "incompetent" is almost always redundant when used as an objection. For instance, a witness may be deemed incompetent to answer a question because he was not personally present at the event he is asked to testify about. In such a case it is only necessary for the objecting attorney to point out that it is hearsay. Objecting on the further grounds that the question or answer is incompetent accomplishes nothing except to make the trial record longer. An attorney can logically object to a question being irrelevant or immaterial, however. The former objection would be proper if the question or answer had no bearing on the case, the latter if it had no importance as evidence.

Some veteran trial lawyers still use this largely meaningless phrase. Younger lawyers are more likely merely to say, "Object as irrelevant" or "Object as immaterial," and seldom use the word "incompetent" at all. They also tend to object on these grounds only when the question or answer is actually irrelevant or immaterial and not to employ the words as a sort of scatter-gun objection in all situations, even when the real ground for objection is something else.

Chapter 2

ROMAN LAW

One of the biggest differences in the field of civil law between the legal systems of primitive societies and those of civilized cultures is that primitive law is usually restricted to compensation for damages, whereas what some legal historians refer to as *mature law* covers a multitude of other things. This is apparent in comparing even the earliest civilizations to primitive societies.

Nearly four thousand years ago in ancient Babylonia the Code of Hammurabi laid down rules concerning barter and trade; fixed fees that could be charged by physicians, various artisans, and transporters of goods or persons; and decreed a number of other business regulations. The Twelve Tables, the earliest known code of Roman law, drawn up by a group of ten magistrates between 451 and 449 B.C., dealt with domestic relations, property, and a number of other purely civil matters in addition to crimes and compensations. (It also laid down some wonderfully quaint rules: For example, no gold other than dental fillings could be buried in graves with deceased persons; plaintiffs were responsible for the transportation to court of ill or aged defendants, but the latter could not insist on any special type of transportation and had to accept even uncushioned carriages if offered.)

Yet contemporary to both the Babylonians and the Romans were numerous barbaric societies in Europe and Asia, none of whose legal systems dealt with any of these matters.

Although modern law derived from many sources, probably the Jewish law of the Bible has been the strongest influence on our criminal law, and Roman law has been the strongest single influence on our civil law. (Canon law has also strongly influenced modern civil law, but except for its original thinking in the fields of marriage, divorce, and probate, canon law also largely derived from Roman law.) The development of Jewish law was gone into in some depth in *Man and Society*. Now we will take a look at Roman law.

The legendary date of the founding of Rome is 753 B.C. The legendary founders were Romulus and Remus, twin sons of the king of Alba Longa, an ancient city near Rome. The brothers were supposed to have led a group of colonists from their father's city to the site of the seven hills, where they established a new city.

During the so-called regal period legend has it that there were seven kings. Romulus is said to have ruled for thirty-eight years, until 715 B.C. The last king, Lucius Tarquinius Superbus, was a tyrant who was overthrown in 510 B.C. All these dates are largely guesses by historians, as the history of the period was handed down by word of mouth instead of in writing, but they are considered reasonably accurate.

After the ousting of Tarquinius Superbus a republican form of government was established. Under the republic, rule was by two elected *praetores,* later called *consules.* The two *praetores* shared joint authority and ruled with the advice of a senate and an assembly. They were elected annually and could serve only one term.

Under the seven kings Rome had been merely an independent city. Under the republic it began to expand into the surrounding countryside. In 264 B.C., when it ruled a good part of the Italian peninsula, Rome made its first move toward eventual world domination by going to war with the North African state of Carthage over control of the Mediterranean Sea. When the Punic Wars ended in 146 B.C., Rome was an empire. It was nearly another century and a quarter before anyone attained the title of emperor, though. In 45 B.C. Julius Caesar was made dictator for life, which gave him as much power as some future emperors, but his heir, Augustus, who ruled from 27 B.C. to A.D. 14, was the first to hold the actual title of emperor. Thereafter emperors ruled for the next 462 years. Thus Roman law developed under four different forms of government: a kingdom, a republic, a limited dictatorship, and an absolute monarchy.

About all we know of ancient Roman law predating the republic is that it had its origins in the customs of various clans. Each clan included a specific number of families, and the head of each family was a clan elder. The elders served as both legislators and judges, and the clan head often wore four hats: He was chief judge, chief priest, political leader, and commander in battle. The clans that joined together to form Rome brought with them their *jus gentilitalis* (literally "the law of the gentiles," a gentile in this case not being a non-Jew but merely a member of the clan). Originally clan members were subject only to the laws of their own clan, but the problems resulting from a dozen separate systems of law in the same community eventually caused a merger of the various systems into one applicable to all citizens.

Even after the merger there was by no means uniformity of justice for all citizens, though. There were two classes of citizens: patricians, or nobles, and plebeians, or the common people. It is not known just how the two classes developed, but it is generally theorized that when the various clans decided to combine their laws into a single comprehensive system, the more powerful clans mutually agreed that certain preferential legal rights would apply only to members of their clans and not to members of the weaker clans. Thus only patricians could vote, become priests, or have contracts enforced. Until, under the republic, the lower class managed to gain at least a few more rights, plebeians had almost as few rights as slaves. They could not own property, bring suit in court, or even contract marriage. As a result only patricians were of legitimate birth.

In 451 B.C., under the republic, the Senate appointed the *Decemviri* ("the Ten Men") to collect Roman law into a code. The result was the previously mentioned Twelve Tables, completed two years later. The Twelve Tables, although not a statement of rights such as the English Magna Charta, was as important to future Roman law as the Magna Charta was to subsequent English law. It merely consolidated existing law instead of making new law but there was one major innovation. It extended the law to all citizens equally.

Actually this extension was largely theoretical at that time, and as a practical matter patricians continued to have many rights denied to plebeians. A plebeian, for example, could not bring suit against a patrician, but a patrician could hale a plebeian into court. The code did make it easier for plebeians to deal with each other in legal matters, however. Not until about the time of the destruction of Carthage in 146 B.C., ending the Third Punic War and heralding the beginning of Rome's conquest of the entire known world, did plebeians gain actual equality before the law.

Meantime Rome had gradually developed from a simple, self-contained agricultural economy into a highly developed capitalistic empire whose economy depended on the complex interdependence of agriculture, industry, manufacturing, shipping, and trade. It had been necessary for the law to develop along with it, and the changes in civil law were as enormous as those in the economy. Many of the developments influenced the later development of English law and eventually of United States law. The two most lasting influences of Roman law on both Continental and English law were in the fields of contracts and torts (civil wrongs), but Rome was also responsible for a couple of legal devices that persist to this day: the *injunction* and the *attachment*.

The injunction was a tremendously sophisticated step forward from primitive law toward mature law in that it is a device designed to prevent wrong before it happens. An injunction is a court writ issued by a magistrate ordering someone either to cease or to refrain from committing some particular act. An example will probably make this clearer. Your neighbor tells you he plans to dig a drainage ditch on his property. You decide that the ditch may undermine a dividing rock wall you have built between the two properties. You obtain a court injunction forbidding him to dig the ditch until an engineer has evaluated its possible effect on your wall. Even though the inconvenience of having to hire an engineer may anger your neighbor, it is obviously better for all concerned for the possible collapse of your wall to be avoided than for you to have to sue for damages after the harm has been done. If your neighbor ignores the court injunction and goes ahead with his ditch without first consulting an engineer, he will be in trouble even if it develops that your fears were groundless and no damage occurred to your wall. The judge who issued him the injunction may find him in contempt of court and either fine or imprison him or do both.

An attachment is a court order to seize the goods or property of a debtor in order to enforce the payment of the debt. Today, in the United States, such seizures are usually made by sheriffs or marshals, after which the goods or property is sold at public auction. After the deduction of costs the debt is paid from the proceeds of the auction; then the balance, if any, is turned over to the person whose property was seized.

In Rome it was possible to obtain an attachment not only against goods but also against the debtor's person, if his goods were of insufficient value to satisfy the judgment. The debtor could then be held in custody until his family or friends ransomed him by paying his debt. This custom carried over into Continental and English law and was eventually imported to the United States, where debtors' prisons flourished into the nineteenth century. In both England and the United States, statutes have long since barred imprisonment for debt, however.

Roman law was also responsible for the system of *equity*. In all modern nations the law of the land in criminal matters applies to all persons within its boundaries, whether they are citizens or aliens, with the exception of certain persons granted diplomatic immunity under treaty arrangements. In most modern nations the civil courts are also available to anyone who has a claim falling under their jurisdiction, regardless of citizenship. A Parisian inventor, for instance, can sue a Los Angeles corporation either in a United States district court or in the California courts for nonpayment of agreed-upon royalties. As will be explained in more detail in Chapter 3, the United States district courts are the general trial courts of the United States government and are available to the plaintiff on the grounds that the suit is a diversity of citizenship case—that is, a controversy between a citizen and an alien. The state court is also available to him, if he prefers, because contracts are subject to state law.

In Rome the *jus civile,* or civil law, applied to citizens only. When Rome, as the world center of trade, began to attract alien businessmen from all over the world, something had to be done to protect their legal interests. Initially these *peregrini* (friendly aliens, as distinguished from *hostes,* or enemy aliens) were allowed to use the laws of their own countries to some extent. Some managed to get themselves under the special protection of patricians, who handled their legal affairs by proxy in their own names.

Neither alternative was very satisfactory, though. The simple solution would have been merely to apply the law equally to all who came before the bar, regardless of citizenship, but Roman citizenship was a jealously guarded privilege, and the government was unwilling to allow it to lose any of its importance by extending to noncitizens any of its prerogatives. There was also the factor that a good deal of Roman law had religious origins, and most of the *peregrini* were not believers in the Roman gods.

The Roman solution was to create a new type of magistrate titled the *praetor peregrinus* to sit on cases involving aliens. He applied what was called *jus gentium,* or the law of aliens. Originally *jus gentium* was supposed to be the law of the alien involved in the action or if two aliens of different nations were involved, a combination of the law of both lands. Since the magistrate wasn't necessarily familiar with the foreign law, however, in actual practice it was usually merely what he assumed the alien law was or sometimes merely what the more convincing of the litigants had persuaded him it was.

In 106 B.C. one of Rome's greatest orators, statesmen, and scholars, Marcus Tullius Cicero, was born. Cicero lived until the time of Julius Caesar. As a matter of fact he outlived Caesar by one year, dying in 43 B.C. During his long and illustrious career he made numerous contributions to legal scholarship, but perhaps his greatest single contribution was the doctrine of *jus naturale,* or natural law.

The doctrine of natural law was not entirely original with Cicero but was merely refined and elaborated on by him from a principle of Greek law. Somewhat oversimplified, the concept is that all law has perpetually existed, whether ever enacted or not. Therefore it is possible for judges to "discover" an appropriate law in any case where no actual statute applies. This concept can get a little sticky if you try to imagine what the "natural law" concerning the use of radio and television broadcast bands was during the Middle Ages, but it was quite helpful in the development of equity.

The *praetores peregrini* began to apply Cicero's doctrine to cases where alien law either was unknown to the magistrate or didn't adequately apply to the matter at hand. The concept gave them almost unlimited leeway in finding a law to fit any situation. With this freedom to virtually ignore written law, the *praetores peregrini* soon fell into the habit of attempting to arrive at the fairest decision possible by *aequitas,* which simply means "reasonableness." The word *equity* derives from *aequitas.*

Jus gentium became so flexible in comparison to the rigid civil law that Roman citizens began to realize that foreign merchants were obtaining a higher standard of justice than they were. Public clamor eventually forced the civil courts to adopt much of the same procedures as the *praetores peregrini.* This did not usurp the civil law but constituted a second type of law practiced side by side with the old law in the same courtroom. *Aequitas* could be applied in cases where the magistrate deemed the law itself inadequate to do justice.

When Roman law began to be revived at the end of the feudal period, this principle reappeared in English common law. When a litigant felt that the inflexible rules of procedure in the regular courts had denied him justice, he could appeal to the king's chancellor. If the appeal seemed to have merit, the chancellor would appoint a special chancery court to consider the matter solely on the basis of *equity,* without regard to what the law was.

The concept of equity was brought to America from England. After the Revolution a number of states established chancery courts in addition to their regular courts. By the time of the Civil War most such courts had been abolished and equity was vested in the regular courts, just as it had been during the Roman Empire. Five states still maintain separate chancery courts, though: Arkansas, Delaware, Mississippi, Tennessee, and Vermont. In the other forty-five states, where the regular courts have the dual power to administer both law and equity, lawyers sometimes speak of bringing action in the "law side" or the "equity side" of the court.

A number of states have attempted to abolish the distinction between law and equity, without complete success, by classing all civil actions as *legal,* regardless of their nature. Other states still distinguish between *legal* and *equitable* actions. Actually all that has really been accomplished in those states where the term *equity* is no longer used is that the terminology has been changed, since actions formerly classed as equitable are still brought in the same manner in the same courts. In general, in those states where the term *equity* is still used, *legal* actions include such things as suits asking for money judgments or the recovery of property, breach of contract, and damage suits. *Equitable* actions include such things as requesting an accounting from the executor of an estate, demanding specific performance of a contract, and requesting an injunction.

After the fall of the Roman Empire toward the end of the fifth century, law everywhere in Europe and in England underwent increasingly rapid change. The tribal law of the Franks adulterated, and in some localities entirely replaced, the Roman law in western Germany and northern France. The Burgundians brought their tribal law to southern France; the Visigoths took theirs to Spain; the Lombards imported theirs into Italy. When the Anglo-Saxons overran England, they didn't just adulterate the Roman law. They totally abolished it and substituted their own Germanic tribal law. On the Continent Roman-law traditions lingered on much longer than in England, but eventually Germanic customs came to prevail there too. During the age of feudalism Roman law virtually disappeared. Toward the end of the eleventh century there was a revival of Roman law resulting from a number of different factors. One was the rediscovery by scholars of a great legal work known as the *Corpus Juris Civilis*.

When Emperor Theodosius I died in A.D. 395, each of his two sons inherited half the empire. Arcadius became emperor of the eastern half, whose capital was Constantinople; Honorius ruled the western half from Rome. The empire had been partitioned and reunited a couple of times previously, but this was its final and permanent division into two separate empires. The Eastern Empire continued to flourish long after the last western emperor was deposed in A.D. 476. Eventually becoming known as the Byzantine Empire, it survived until conquered by the Turks in 1453.

In A.D. 528 Emperor Justinian I, of the Eastern Empire, also known as Justinian the Great, ordered all Roman law compiled into a single massive work that eventually became known as the *Corpus Juris Civilis*. In 544 the Eastern Empire reconquered Italy and part of Spain (also a portion of North Africa, but that has no bearing on the development of law in Europe). Since Justinian had decreed that the law of the *Corpus Juris Civilis* was to be in effect throughout the empire, it was introduced in the newly conquered territories. After Justinian's death in 565, however, the Lombards took over Italy, and the Visigoths drove the Byzantines out of Spain. Both imposed their own tribal law on the populace, and the *Corpus Juris Civilis* became merely a manuscript in the libraries of a few monasteries.

Toward the end of the eleventh century the compilation was rediscovered by scholars in northern Italy and began to be taught in the Italian universities. The university at Bologna became the best-known law school in Europe, and during the early part of the twelfth century a legal professor on its staff named Irnerius became the most famous lecturer on the *Corpus Juris Civilis*. Students began to flock to Bologna from all over Europe to study under him and then take their knowledge of the *Corpus Juris Civilis* back to their own countries.

The revival of knowledge of Roman law did not instantly result in a revival of its practice, of course, but it did result in considerable influence on feudal law. This influence was strongest and took place most quickly in the Germanic nations of the so-called Holy Roman Empire. Frederick I Barbarossa, toward the end of the twelfth century, attempted to impose the *Corpus Juris Civilis* as the universal law throughout the empire, and subsequent emperors attempted the same thing, none with more than partial success.

The reason the emperors of the Holy Roman Empire accepted the *Corpus Juris Civilis* so enthusiastically was that they nurtured the fantasy that their empire was the direct descendant of the Western Empire of Rome and that they were the legal successors of the Roman emperors. They therefore argued that imperial law was still in effect because the Roman Empire had never died. Nobody but the emperors themselves really subscribed to this grandiose idea, though. Actually the empire was merely an extremely loose federation of independent kingdoms over which the emperor had little real control and whose kings had little more control over their virtually independent barons. Voltaire said the Holy Roman Empire was "neither holy, Roman, nor an empire." Some barons accepted the *Corpus Juris Civilis* when it suited their own interests to do so; others simply ignored the imperial decrees.

Nevertheless the *Corpus Juris Civilis* strongly influenced Continental law. Nowhere did it completely supplant local law, but it had varying degrees of effect on existing law nearly everywhere in Europe, and eventually in England. In general its strongest influences were in the areas of contracts and torts, and it had lesser influence on laws concerning property. It had no effect whatever on marriage and divorce laws, where canon law remained supreme, nor did it influence inheritance laws, which continued to be shaped largely by Germanic and feudal traditions.

The *Corpus Juris Civilis* was unknown to the Anglo-Saxons of England. When William the Conqueror arrived there in 1066, he brought the feudal law of Normandy with him. He did not abolish local law but merely superimposed Norman law on top of it. Subsequently English students traveled to Bologna to study under Irnerius, just as students from other European countries did, and brought back to England knowledge of Roman law. Eventually the three merged into English common law, and since American law is a direct linear descendant of English common law, the influence of the Romans on our civil law has been as strong as it was in England.

Chapter 3

THE CIVIL COURTS

FEDERAL COURTS

There are three levels of federal courts in the United States, plus some specialized courts called *legislative courts*.

(1) The trial courts in which federal crimes are tried and which also have original jurisdiction over civil actions triable on the federal level are called United States district courts. The United States and its possessions are divided into ninety-one federal judicial districts, in each of which is a district court.

(2) Above these are the United States courts of appeal, which review cases tried in the district courts when there are grounds for appeal. Prior to 1948 these were called circuit courts of appeal. There are eleven judicial circuits, each having a court of appeal.

(3) Decisions of the courts of appeal may be appealed to the United States Supreme Court, the highest court in the nation.

The Constitution limits the jurisdiction of the federal courts to the following types of cases: (1) those arising under the Constitution, the laws of the United States, or treaties made with other countries; (2) those affecting ambassadors, other public ministers, and consuls; (3) admiralty and maritime cases; (4) controversies in which the United States is a party; (5) controversies between states or between states and the citizens of other states; (6) controversies between citizens of different states (called *diversity of citizenship* cases, a term that also includes controversies between citizens and aliens); (7) controversies between citizens of the same state involving land grants of different states; and (8) controversies between states or citizens with foreign nations or citizens. These limits are not as rigid as they may first seem, because they appear in the Constitution more in the nature of suggested guidelines for Congress to follow than as actual restrictions. Article III, Section 1, of the Constitution states: "The judicial power of the United States shall be vested in one Supreme Court, and in such inferior courts as *the Congress may from time to time ordain and establish* [italics mine]."

Aside from stipulating that there should be a Supreme Court, the Constitution thus left the construction of the federal court system to Congress. Even the actual composition of the Supreme Court was left to Congress, which has from time to time varied the number of justices from six to eleven. For the past hundred years the number has remained at nine, but there is nothing in the Constitution to prevent Congress from changing the Court to any size it desires at any time it wishes. As a matter of practical politics it would be exceedingly difficult for Congress to make such a change, because the proponents of such a change would be accused by its opponents of political motivation. In most cases the charge would quite obviously be correct, as the most probable reason for suggesting a decreased number of justices would be to get rid of one whose philosophy was opposed to that of the proponents and the most probable reason for

wanting an increased number would be to allow the
President to pack the court with justices who hold his
political philosophy.

The Judiciary Act of 1789 created the federal court
system, and subsequent judiciary acts have only slightly revised the original organization. The same act defined the jurisdiction of the various courts, using the
Constitutional list as a guide but varying from it
enough to establish the point that Congress considered
it only a guide. In passing the act, Congress made it
quite clear that the federal courts, created by *Congress* rather than by the Constitution, must also look
to Congress instead of to the Constitution for their
jurisdictional powers.

The only jurisdictional matters over which Congress
has no control are cases affecting ambassadors, other
public ministers, and consuls, those in which a state is
a party, and admiralty and maritime cases. The Constitution specifically states that the Supreme Court has
original jurisdiction in all but the last of these categories, which means that it acts as a trial court instead of as an appeal court in such cases. Admiralty
and maritime cases are tried in the lower federal courts.

As to the other classes of cases listed in the Constitution as within the "judicial power of the United
States," Congress has used its own discretion. Thus diversity of citizenship cases, despite being listed in the
Constitution as properly falling under the federal jurisdiction, cannot be tried in federal courts unless a certain minimum amount of money is involved. Congress,
in its various judiciary acts, has changed the statutory
amount from time to time, but currently it is ten
thousand dollars. An attempt to allow suits for lower
amounts in actions by consumers against manufac-

turers only was defeated by the 1970 Congress. So, with certain minor exceptions such as maritime cases and, more recently, a piece of legislation known as the Miller Act which grants federal employees the right to use the federal courts for suits less than ten thousand dollars, all civil suits involving less than that amount, even though between citizens of different states or between United States citizens and foreigners, must be instituted in state courts.

The Judiciary Act of 1789 also does not give automatic jurisdiction to federal courts even in cases involving Constitutional provisions or federal laws of treaties unless one or more of these matters are central to the case. If the Constitutional provision or law or treaty is merely of peripheral importance, without bearing on the main issue, neither party has the right to move the case under federal jurisdiction. Since the Constitution requires the judges of the state courts to abide by the Constitution, they are deemed to be as capable as federal judges to render decisions in such matters. If either side objects to the rulings of such state judges and has proper legal grounds for such objection, there is, of course, the right to appeal to the federal courts.

Even when Congress clearly vested jurisdiction in the federal courts, jurisdiction was not necessarily withdrawn from the state courts. In many of the areas mentioned in the Constitution, *concurrent jurisdiction* is held by both state and federal courts. For example, in a suit for ten thousand dollars or more in damages brought by a Californian against a resident of New York State, the action can be started by the plaintiff either in federal court or in the general trial court of the state where the damage is alleged to have been inflicted (unless the damage is the result of a traffic accident, when special rules apply that will be covered later). Customarily it is the latter. The defendant, in most circumstances, can have the case removed to a federal court if he wishes, but it is seldom done. If there is no particular advantage to either side in having such a case tried in federal court instead of in a state court, there is no point in insisting on it.

In the District of Columbia there are no courts equivalent to the general trial courts of the states. The United States district court there consequently serves in that capacity in cases that normally would be heard in the state courts in addition to fulfilling its federal functions. In the four United States territories of Puerto Rico, the Canal Zone, Guam, and the Virgin Islands there are certain inferior territorial courts but again no courts equivalent to the states' general trial courts. In these four areas the district courts have the same jurisdiction on the federal level as other district courts but by Congressional statute have also been given jurisdiction over local matters, so that, as in the District of Columbia, they also exercise a function similar to state trial courts.

In addition to the three basic federal courts, there are four *legislative courts* on the federal level which deserve at least brief mention.

(1) The United States Court of Claims was created in 1855 for the sole purpose of hearing claims against the federal government. Appeals from its decisions go directly to the Supreme Court instead of first being heard by a United States court of appeal.

(2) The Tax Court of the United States (until 1942 called the Board of Tax Appeals) was created in 1924. It consists of sixteen judges who every two

years vote one of themselves the chief judge. It hears appeals by taxpayers who differ with the Bureau of Internal Revenue about their tax bills. Its rulings are appealable by either side to a United States court of appeal, and from there to the Supreme Court.

(3) The United States Customs Court was created in 1926. (Prior to that a Board of General Appraisers, abolished by the same act that created the Customs Court, performed a somewhat similar function.) The court consists of nine judges appointed by the President, only five of whom may be from the same political party. The President also designates one as chief judge. The Customs Court has a function similar to the Tax Court in that it hears appeals from persons who object to the duties imposed on imported merchandise by collectors of customs. It is required by law to sit in New York City instead of in Washington, D.C., where the other legislative courts sit. Appeals from its decisions go to the Court of Customs and Patent Appeals.

(4) The United States Court of Customs and Patent Appeals was established in 1948 and consists of a chief judge and four associate judges. As its name implies, it hears appeals from persons who have been denied patents in addition to hearing appeals from the Customs Court.

A patent is an exclusive license to use, manufacture, and sell a particular device or procedure for a specified period of time. The head of the United States Patent Office, the United States Commissioner of Patents, grants patents on inventions for seventeen years and on unique designs for existing inventions for periods ranging from three and a half to fourteen years. If the Patent Office refuses to grant a patent for an invention, or the patent granted is more restrictive than the applicant believes it should be, he may appeal to the Patent Office Board of Appeals. This is not a court but is merely an administrative panel within the Patent Office. An adverse decision by the board may be appealed to the Court of Customs and Patent Appeals.

The Supreme Court is empowered to review determinations made by this court, both in customs and patent matters, but in practice so seldom does that for all practical purposes its decisions are final. Part of the reason for this is that the judges of the Court of Customs and Patent Appeals of necessity acquire such highly specialized knowledge in the two fields with which they are solely concerned that the Supreme Court recognizes as a matter of common sense that they are more expert in these matters than the members of the higher court could possibly be. There is also the factor that most rulings by the Court of Customs and Patent Appeals are on matters of fact rather than on matters of law. That is, the court is less concerned with interpretations of the law than with the facts of cases. A ruling that an invention is too similar to one already patented, for instance, is a ruling on a matter of fact. There is no interpretation of the law for the Supreme Court to review.

Violations of patents are not the concern of either the Patent Office or the Court of Customs and Patent Appeals. They are strictly concerned with the granting of patents. A patent-holder who believes his patent is being infringed must bring suit in a United States district court.

STATE COURTS

Each of the fifty states has its own laws, its own court system, and its own court procedures; however, all of the legal systems except that of Louisiana evolved essentially from English common law. Louisiana has a codified system inherited from the French, who once owned it. A codified system of law is one in which at some time or other all the laws of the land were reviewed and were systematically organized into a single code. The code may thereafter be revised by the passage of new laws, but the new laws are fitted into it in the proper places so that it remains a compilation of all law. French law is based on the Code Napoléon, which went into effect in 1804 under Napoleon Bonaparte.

The common heritage of English common law tends to make the systems of the forty-nine states other than Louisiana at least roughly similar. Constitutional limits on the states' legislative and judicial powers, plus the Constitutional provision that the judges of state courts must abide by the Constitution, make even Louisiana courts very similar to the rest despite its codified system. Although there are many minor variations in civil law from state to state, in the main the rules for transacting business, buying and selling property, and bringing lawsuits are very much alike.

The courts and court procedures are very similar too, although there is considerable variation in terminology. All states have general trial courts for the trying of both criminal and civil suits. All have systems of inferior courts below these trial courts which handle misdemeanors and minor civil claims. All have appeal procedures for the review of contested decisions.

In forty-two states the highest state court, like the federal high court, is simply called the supreme court. In three it is called the court of appeals, in two the supreme court of appeals, in two the supreme judicial court, and in one the supreme court of errors.

Thirty-seven states have no intermediate courts of appeal equivalent to the United States courts of appeal on the federal level. In those states cases from the general trial courts are appealed directly to the states' highest courts. Oklahoma has an intermediate appeal court for criminal cases only, civil cases being appealed directly to its supreme court. In the twelve states having intermediate appeals courts for civil cases, eight call them courts of appeal, two call them appellate courts, and one—New York State—calls its intermediate court the appellate division of the supreme court. (The supreme court referred to is not in this case the highest state court. New York added to the confusion of terminology in different states by calling its general trial court the supreme court.) Texas has separate intermediate appeals courts for civil and criminal matters, respectively called the court of civil appeals and the court of criminal appeals.

The most popular name for general trial courts is the circuit court, with seventeen states using it. Next is district court, with sixteen users, then superior court, with fourteen. As mentioned above, New York State calls its trial court the supreme court. Ohio's is the court of common pleas. In Vermont the county courts are the highest general trial courts.

To further confuse things, four states have inferior courts called circuit courts, three have inferior courts called district courts, six have lower courts called courts of common pleas, and four have inferior courts rather incongruously called superior courts. A few other titles for lower courts, picked at random from various states, are civil court of record, court of claims, quarterly court, land court, court of general sessions, commissioners' court, and corporation court.

My personal favorite, because of the way its name seems to ring with judicial authority, has always been Pennsylvania's court of quarter session, oyer and terminer, which became a casualty to modernization in a 1969 reorganization of the Pennsylvania court system. "Oyer" means the hearing of a writ, bond, or other such matter; "terminer" is a noun meaning a determining. Thus a court of oyer and terminer is one constituted to hear and determine matters, usually matters of a criminal nature.

In addition to the above courts, twenty-one states have county courts that are courts of original jurisdiction in both criminal and civil matters.

Now let us take a look in somewhat more detail at the civil court systems of California, New York State, and Missouri. In all three states the highest court consists of a chief justice and six associate justices. In California and Missouri the high court is called the supreme court. In New York State it is the court of appeals.

With some minor differences, the high courts of California and New York State function very much the same. One such difference is that in New York it is possible to appeal cases to the court of appeals even from justice of the peace courts. In California the general trial court (superior court) is the final appeals court for civil cases that arise in both justice and municipal courts, and only in exceptional circum-

STATE COURTS

	CALIFORNIA	MISSOURI	NEW YORK
HIGHEST COURT	supreme court	supreme court	court of appeals
INTERMEDIATE APPEALS COURTS	courts of appeal	courts of appeal	appellate divisions of the supreme court
GENERAL TRIAL COURTS	superior courts departments: probate courts, conciliation courts, juvenile courts, etc.	circuit courts or courts of common pleas	supreme courts
INFERIOR COURTS	municipal and justice courts small-claims courts	magistrate courts, probate courts, county courts	county courts or civil court of the City of New York or district courts; surrogate courts, city courts, justice courts

stances may they be appealed beyond that level. If a case involves a question that either may or has become recurrent throughout the state, a superior court may allow it to be appealed beyond its own jurisdiction in order to have a precedent established by the higher court, or the district court of appeal may order the superior court to send along the trial record for further review for the same reason. One or the other of these is particularly likely to happen if different superior court judges, acting as appellate judges for justice or municipal court cases, have handed down conflicting opinions in similar cases. The higher court might also be induced to review such a case if it involved a matter of widespread interest or importance, such as the legality of a local business license fee of twenty-five dollars.

Another difference is that many more types of cases in New York have "right of appeal" than in California. That is, the high court is required by law to review such cases, whereas in cases reviewable only by "permission" the court has the choice of refusing review. For example, cases in New York State have right of appeal from the appellate division of the supreme court when one or more of the appellate-division judges dissents from the majority opinion or when the appellate division has reversed a lower-court decision. Only when a lower-court decision is confirmed can the court of appeals refuse further review. Despite these differences, though, in general the function of both the California supreme court and the New York State court of appeals is to review cases already reviewed by the intermediate appeals court and then appealed on to them.

In Missouri, on the other hand, there is a division of labor between the state supreme court and the courts of appeal. The supreme court has exclusive appellate jurisdiction in civil cases involving more than fifteen thousand dollars, in cases involving interpretation of the federal or state Constitutions and federal statutes or treaties, in cases involving title to real property, and in a number of other matters. That is, such cases are appealed directly to the supreme court from the trial court instead of first being reviewed by a court of appeal. In the cases the courts of appeal get—money suits involving less than fifteen thousand dollars, for example—they have final appellate jurisdiction, and the cases cannot be appealed to the Missouri supreme court. (They may be appealed to the United States Supreme Court, however.)

Another way in which the Missouri supreme court considerably differs from the highest courts of California and New York is that it has attached to it six commissioners, who are empowered to hear arguments and submit reports to the court. The court may approve, modify, or reject such reports. Approved or modified reports have the same effect as supreme court decisions in which the court itself has heard the arguments.

As in Missouri, California's intermediate appeals court is called the court of appeal. As already mentioned, in New York State it is called the appellate division of the supreme court.

In California there are thirteen courts of appeal, divided among five districts. The two smallest districts have only one court each, and the other three districts have two, four, and five courts. The courts of appeal accept cases for review mainly from only the general trial courts but in certain instances will review cases from municipal and justice courts.

In Missouri there are three appellate districts, each with a court of appeal. In general each has final appellate jurisdiction in its own district of all cases appealed to it from the general trial courts and inferior courts of record, but as mentioned above, its jurisdiction is restricted to those types of cases not appealable directly to the state supreme court.

New York State is divided into four judicial departments, each with an appellate division of the supreme court. They hear appeals not only from the general trial courts but also from county courts, surrogate courts, family courts, courts of claim, and even from administrative agencies. Unlike the courts of appeal in

California and Missouri, they are specifically empowered to review questions of fact as well as of law. (In actual practice the California and Missouri courts also review facts, although they are supposedly restricted to reviewing questions of law only. They accomplish this by the employment of such terminology as "The evidence presented fails to uphold the decision rendered," which is clearly a review of facts under the guise of being merely a review of the lower court's legal interpretation of the evidence.) They also have original jurisdiction in certain cases, which means they act as trial courts instead of as appeals courts. Among such cases are those in which opponents have agreed on the facts and the only issues are those of interpretation of the law, petitions against certain judges, and disbarment proceedings.

The trial courts and inferior courts of the three states vary from each other too much to attempt to compare them on each level, so we will consider them by state.

In California the general trial court is the superior court. Each county has one, with one or more departments, depending on the size of the county. Los Angeles County, the largest in the state, has twelve departments, plus a one-judge court at Inglewood restricted to hearing cases of probate, default, dissolution of marriage, and minor civil matters. Superior courts have jurisdiction in all civil matters not given by law to inferior courts. They also exercise appellate jurisdiction over municipal and justice courts within their jurisdictions.

The various superior courts designate certain of their departments to handle specific matters. Thus California probate courts are merely special departments of superior courts which handle probate matters. Conciliation courts are also specialized departments of some superior courts. They have jurisdiction over controversies between spouses when such controversies threaten to end in dissolution of marriage. Either spouse may invoke the jurisdiction of the court by filing a petition. Usually the court will take cases only when the welfare of a minor may be affected by a breakup of the marriage but in certain situations will accept petitions when there are no children. As the name implies, the function of the court is to affect reconciliation and avoid dissolution of marriage. Another department of the superior court is the juvenile court. Except for the rather large area of dependent children, juvenile court is almost entirely concerned with criminal matters.

In California the type of inferior court a community has depends on its population. A few counties have consolidated municipal courts that are county-wide and therefore include even the smallest communities in their jurisdiction, but most counties are divided into judicial districts. Each district with a population of more than forty thousand has a municipal court. Those with less than forty thousand have justice courts.

Municipal courts have jurisdiction in civil cases involving cash or property of value up to five thousand dollars, except in cases involving taxes or title to real property. The superior court has jurisdiction in those cases, regardless of amount. Justice courts have civil jurisdiction in small-claims cases only, for amounts not exceeding five hundred dollars. A small-claims court with the same ceiling is also a part of each municipal court. This small-claims court does not have a separate presiding judge, the judge of the municipal court also acting as small-claims judge. In small-claims cases neither side is represented by an attorney.

In Missouri the general trial court is called the circuit court. It has original jurisdiction over all civil matters except probate and those matters given by law to magistrate courts (the Missouri equivalent to California's municipal and justice courts). In certain cases the circuit courts also have concurrent jurisdiction with magistrate courts—for instance when opposing parties to an action that normally would be the business of the inferior court are from different counties. Circuit courts have appellate jurisdiction over magistrate courts, probate courts, and county courts.

In two areas of Missouri there are courts of common pleas which are on the same judicial level as the circuit courts. One, in Cape Girardeau County, exercises concurrent jurisdiction with the county's circuit court in all areas except one and ousts the circuit court in that area. This exception is that the court of common pleas has superintending control over the magistrate courts of that county, a function of the circuit courts elsewhere in the state.

The other court of common pleas is at Mark Twain's birthplace, Hannibal. It has jurisdiction in only two townships of Marion County and takes the place of a circuit court. Like circuit courts everywhere else in Missouri except in Cape Girardeau County, the court of common pleas at Hannibal has original jurisdiction in all criminal and civil matters except those delegated to inferior courts and has appellate jurisdiction over magistrate courts.

These two courts, hangovers from an earlier day, somehow managed to resist the unification in the court system undertaken in Missouri some years ago. They are mentioned primarily to show that the court systems of all states are not organized with the same degree of efficiency. There are such odd appendages to otherwise orderly and streamlined court systems in a number of our states.

Unlike California, the Missouri probate courts are not merely departments of the general trial courts but are separate courts. They have jurisdiction over all probate matters, appoint guardians for minors and persons of unsound mind, and act on all other matters concerning estates and wills. There is one such court in each county.

Magistrate courts in Missouri are of two classes, the higher roughly corresponding to California municipal courts, the lower roughly comparing to California justice courts. In counties with a population under four hundred thousand, magistrate courts have original jurisdiction in civil actions involving no more than $2,000. In larger counties they have jurisdiction up to $3,500. Both classes have exclusive jurisdiction, which means their decisions are not appealable, in cases involving amounts of less than $50.

An odd bit of legislation gives magistrate courts original jurisdiction in one area, regardless of the amount involved. This is in actions against railroads operating in the state when the action is solely to recover damages for killing or injuring livestock or other animals. Thus a suit for as much as $100,000 against a railroad for the death of a prize bull or a racehorse has to be heard in a magistrate court.

The number of magistrate courts in a county depends on the population of the county. In those under 30,000, the probate judge is also the magistrate. Where the population is over 30,000 but less than 70,000, there is one separate magistrate court. Two are authorized for counties with populations between 70,000 and 100,000. One more is added for each 100,000 over the first 100,000.

Missouri also has what it calls county courts, but they bear little resemblance to the courts that bear that title in most other states. In Missouri the county courts are not trial courts. They merely control and manage the property belonging to the county, buy and sell property for it, and audit and settle any demands against the county.

In New York State the general trial court, the afore-mentioned supreme court, has general jurisdiction in law and equity in all matters not specifically delegated to other courts. Throughout the state there are more than two hundred supreme court judges.

In each county, except those within the City of New York, there is a county court. These are considerably more important than the county courts of nearly all other states except Vermont, where the county courts are the only general trial courts. In New York they have concurrent jurisdiction with supreme courts in criminal matters and in actual practice try most serious crimes. In civil matters the courts of the forty-five largest counties have jurisdiction in actions involving money or property valued up to $10,000. In the seventeen smaller counties the ceiling is $6,000. They also have jurisdiction over the sale or disposition of property within the county belonging to infants or incompetents for whom the supreme court has appointed guardians (called *committees* in New York State, even when the committee consists of only one person). County courts also have appellate jurisdiction from judgments of justice courts in which the amounts involved exceed $250.

Each county has a surrogate's court that performs

the same function as the probate courts in California and Missouri. Most of these, as in Missouri, are separate courts, but a few are parts of trial courts, as in California. In counties with a population of less than forty thousand the county judge also acts as surrogate. The law permits but does not specifically require separate surrogate judges in larger counties, with the result that some have them, but in others the county judge wears both hats. In counties of over four hundred thousand the legislature has in some cases provided for the election of separate surrogate judges, but in others it has conferred the powers and jurisdiction of surrogate judges upon the elected judges of the supreme court.

In some areas there are district courts, with jurisdiction over only a portion of a county. These function the same as the county courts in the smaller counties, with jurisdiction in civil actions up to six thousand dollars.

New York is one of the few states that has a court of claims similar to the federal court of the same title. It consists of sixteen judges, one designated as the presiding judge, appointed by the governor, with the consent of the state senate, for terms of nine years. The court has jurisdiction in all claims against the state and in counter-claims by the state against claimants.

The civil court of the City of New York takes the place of a county court in that city. It has much the same jurisdiction as county courts, with some extra powers due to conditions unique to the country's largest city. Like county courts in the larger counties, it has jurisdiction in civil actions up to ten thousand dollars, but it also has jurisdiction, regardless of amount, in rental and eviction cases, issues injunctions to enforce health laws, and presides in many other types of cases stemming from the problems of congested living conditions.

Throughout the state in the various municipalities there are numerous city, municipal, police, and recorders' courts having limited local civil and criminal jurisdiction. Their organizations and jurisdictions are not established by state legislation, however, but by their city charters. Although all have the legal approval of the state in that their city's charters were granted by the state, they vary so widely in their powers that no general description of them is possible other than that their jurisdiction is limited to areas where state law has not granted original jurisdiction to other courts.

As in California, the lowest civil courts in New York State are justice courts. Each town has a justice court limited to jurisdiction in civil actions to amounts not exceeding one thousand dollars. This limit does not apply in rendering judgment for rents due, however, on which there is no limit.

In a few areas the state also has small-claims courts, where actions for money only may be brought when the amount does not exceed three hundred dollars. There is one small-claims court in each borough of New York City as part of the civil court of the City of New York. Small-claims courts are parts of the district courts in most of the districts of Nassau and Suffolk counties also. In other communities throughout the state such minor actions are handled by justices of the peace as part of their regular calendar, without their sitting as special small-claims judges.

Chapter 4

ACTIONS IN LAW

In criminal law the statutes passed by federal and state legislatures sharply limit the types of criminal actions possible, as no one can be tried in the criminal courts unless charged with the violation of a specific statute. In civil law there are no such statutory limits on the types of actions that can be brought. The plaintiff in a civil suit may charge that the defendant has violated some law, but then again no law violation may be involved at all. The criterion is not necessarily the legality of whatever it is the defendant has done that has caused the plaintiff to bring action but rather its effect on the plaintiff. Thus it is not necessary for the plaintiff to prove that the defendant has violated some statute but only that he has caused injury to the plaintiff.

This does not mean that every imagined grievance can get a hearing. Many frivolous claims are summarily dismissed by judges. It does mean that possible causes of action are not limited by the laws on the books. It is not a rare occurrence at all to read in the newspapers that somewhere in the country a unique suit has been brought in which the plaintiff asks relief for a situation that has no legal precedent.

As a random example, in August of 1971 actress Katharine Hepburn filed suit against the manufacturers of Vita herring and its advertising agency, Solow-Weston, Inc., for four million dollars for damaging her reputation and causing her to suffer "great humiliation and stress." Her objection was to a radio commercial featuring "Harriet Hubert Herring, one of the great herring experts of our time," who sang the praises of fish. The actress claimed the Harriet character sounded like her, and as a result the defendants had let the public think she had "stooped to perform below her class, stature, prestige, and prominence."

Throughout the history of show business impersonators have been imitating prominent persons without fear of damage suits so long as they were careful not to defame the characters of those they imitated, because it has been a generally accepted legal principle that persons in the public eye were legitimate subjects for satire. Miss Hepburn's suit claims that impersonation for commercial reasons is quite a different matter than imitation merely to amuse an audience, however. Hers is the first suit for this particular type of damage. As this is written, the suit is still unsettled, but the radio commercial has been taken off the air.

Although it is impossible to list every conceivable cause of action, civil actions do fall into certain more or less specific categories. For convenience I have divided them into two main categories, each of which has a number of subcategories. The two main categories are actions in law and actions in equity.

As was previously mentioned, in some states the distinction between the two is no longer recognized by the courts, but even in those states lawyers still tend to think in terms of certain cases being actions in law (or legal actions, as they are called in some localities) and other cases being actions in equity. In any event the division is convenient for explaining the various types of actions brought in the civil courts. We will begin with actions in law.

ACTIONS TO ENFORCE PAYMENT OF DEBT

The most common action of this type is one in which the creditor requests a money judgment against the debtor for money loaned to him, for goods delivered, or for services rendered. A bank sues to collect on an unsecured personal note. (An unsecured note is one on which the borrower has pledged no security in case of default. Most banks will loan up to five hundred dollars to good risks on signature only, without demanding a lien against the borrower's car or other property. Where there is such a lien, the bank could simply foreclose on the property instead of asking for a money judgment.) A department store asks judgment against a customer who has not paid his charge account. A bakery sues a restaurant that refuses to pay for bread delivered to it. A house painter sues a homeowner who signed a contract for his house to be painted, then refused to pay when the job was done. If the debtor in the first case does not dispute having borrowed the money, or in the second and third cases does not dispute having received the goods, the cases are fairly simple. In the majority of such cases the debtor, having no real defense, simply fails to appear, and the plaintiff is granted judgment by default.

The fourth case may be equally simple, but not necessarily. It becomes slightly complicated if the defendant claims he refused to pay the bill because the quality of the paint job was unsatisfactory. In this case the court must examine the contract, interpret its terms, then receive evidence as to the quality of the job done. Not infrequently in such litigations the opposing lawyers will work out a compromise settlement before the case actually gets to trial—or sometimes during the trial—wherein the creditor agrees to settle for a reduced sum. If the case is fought all the way through in court, the judge—or the jury, if there is one—may grant a judgment for such a reduced amount also.

Actions to enforce payment of debt can become considerably more complicated than this, though. Consider, for instance, the case of the dissolution of partnership in the Goodwald Auto Repairs Company, of Lackawanna, New York. The business was started as an equal partnership in 1965 by John Goodwin and Arthur Oswald, and the company name was formed by using part of each partner's name. Each partner put up $6,000; they signed a two-year lease on a building and equipped it as an auto-repair garage.

The business did not thrive. At the end of the first year they attempted to sell out, but there were no takers. They struggled along another year until their lease ran out, then closed down. They didn't go bankrupt; they merely went out of business.

Arthur Oswald planned to open an automotive-supply store and therefore agreed to accept the garage's supply of spare parts as a portion of his share of the business assets. The value of the spare parts was mutually agreed to be $1,200. John Goodwin had obtained a job in the local Bethlehem steel plant but planned to continue to do part-time automotive-repair work in the back yard of his house. He therefore kept all the hand tools, plus some jacks, as part of his share of the assets. He and his partner agreed that $1,000 was a fair value for the tools.

The remaining assets, consisting of some heavier equipment and a tow truck, were sold for $4,500. Oswald received $2,150 of this, Goodwin $2,350. No contract was drawn up concerning the disposition of any of these assets. Everything was by oral agreement.

Then Arthur Oswald decided not to open an automotive-supply store after all. He sold the spare parts for $2,400. Meantime John Goodwin had taken the painted business sign reading "GOODWALD AUTO REPAIRS" from over the door of the now-vacant repair garage and had fixed it to the roof of his garage at home.

Goodwin demanded $600 from Oswald as his rightful share of the additional amount his partner had obtained for the spare parts over and above their originally agreed-upon value. Oswald countered that the tools kept by Goodwin actually had double the value placed on them by mutual agreement. He also charged that by putting up their old business sign on his home garage, Goodwin in effect was still conducting the same business in a new location, and Oswald was entitled to some compensation for the goodwill value of the sign.

A lawsuit eventually developed, with each ex-partner asking for a money judgment against the other. It was tried in the county court of Erie County, New York. Obviously this was a much more complicated case than the usual action to enforce payment of debt, in which there is generally little question either as to which party is the debtor or as to the amount of the debt. In this case the court had to decide both the amount due and which litigant was to get it.

The case was tried without jury. The judge decided that $1,000 had been a fair value to place on the tools kept by Goodwin, and that Goodwin was entitled to $600 from the sale of the spare parts; however, Oswald in turn was entitled to $500 for the intangible factor of "goodwill" that the use of the old company sign gave to his ex-partner. The court held that removal of the sign at this late date would not cancel out this goodwill factor, because in effect the community had been thoroughly informed by the sign of the location change. The mental convolutions gone through to arrive at the $500 figure for goodwill were not revealed by the judge when he handed down the judgment of $100 against Arthur Oswald. Judges and juries are constantly confronted with the problem of placing an exact monetary value on such intangibles, and as often as not they seem to pluck a figure out of the air.

As complicated as this case may seem, it is actually a relatively simple example of this type of action. Often in the dissolution of partnerships the disposal of assets and the fair distribution of the proceeds is so complicated that the partners take the matter to court for settlement even if the dissolution is taking place on the friendliest of terms, simply because it is too complicated for them to figure out themselves. In some states this is called an *action for an accounting,* in others a *proceeding for an accounting.* This kind of action is not limited to dissolutions of partnership but is also used to require an accounting from persons who have been entrusted with funds belonging to others, such as the trustees of trust funds and the administrators of estates.

Another type of action to enforce payment of debt is the *enforcement of lien.* A lien is a monetary claim against an item of property, either real or personal. The commonest form of lien is the real-estate mortgage. To illustrate how the mortgage works, I will describe an actual transaction of my own.

In August of 1970 I purchased a city lot for investment purposes for $5,400. I paid $1,080 down, leaving a balance of $4,320. As the seller wanted the balance in cash, I obtained a mortgage on the property from my bank for $4,320 at 6 percent interest and paid him off in full. (The availability of this interest rate was the prime factor in my making the investment, because usual mortgage interest rates at that time were 8 to 9 percent.) Under the terms of the mortgage agreement I was to pay back the $4,320, plus accrued interest, in fifty monthly installments of $97.20 each and a final installment of $37.80.

The unpaid balance of the mortgage at any time until it is paid in full constitutes the lien the bank has against this property. The amount of the lien accordingly decreases from month to month by the portion of the payment which applies against the principal, and that portion increases as the lien gets smaller. The first payment of $97.20 reduces the lien by $75.60 only, the other $21.60 being the interest payment. By the time of the twenty-fifth payment $85.21 applies against the principal, and only $11.99 is for interest; $37.61 of the final payment of $37.80 applies on the principal, and only $0.19 is for interest.

If at any time before the mortgage is fully paid off, I stop making payments and the bank concludes that I do not intend to resume them, it may ask the court for a *judgment of foreclosure*. (This would be a last resort, as lending agencies do not like to foreclose if they can avoid it. First the bank would exhaust such possibilities as suggesting refinancing to reduce the size of the payments or finding a buyer willing to take over the mortgage.) If the judgment is granted, the property would be sold at public auction. In order to protect its interests the bank would have a representative present at the auction who would bid in if there was no bid high enough to pay off the mortgage. If no

one topped that bid, the bank would become owner
of the property and could sell it on the open market
for whatever it could get.

Regardless of who ended up owning the property,
out of the amount received from the auction the bank
would receive the amount of the lien and I would be
given the balance, if any, less court costs and other
costs. If the bank was the purchaser, of course, there
would be no balance due me, because its bid would
be only enough to pay off the mortgage, and I would
have no claim on any part of the profit made by the
bank from subsequent sale. With minor variations
(e.g., some states allow the auctioneer to require an
opening bid of a minimum amount), this procedure is
the same for all states.

If it happened that I had many other creditors, all
clamoring for payment of debts, one or more of them
might obtain liens against this property also, up to the
amount of my equity in it, but these claims could not
encroach on the rights of the mortgage-holder. His
right to recover the full amount of his lien against the
property before any other creditor gets paid is absolute. The reason for this is that the lien actually implies part ownership of the property. Another creditor
—say, the Internal Revenue Service—therefore would
have no more right to seize the property and sell it
without paying off the lien than they would have the
right to seize my neighbor's house to satisfy a debt
of mine. Of course, if the property is purchased at
auction for a price higher than the amount of the mortgage, the additional money would apply against these
subsequent liens in the order that they had been filed.

In some cases there is a second or even a third mortgage against property. This occurs most often when the
buyer lacks the money for a down payment. Say the

purchase price of a house is $20,000, and the buyer's bank is willing to grant a mortgage of only $18,000. The buyer may go to another lending agency and take out a second mortgage for $2,000, usually at a higher interest rate.

In the event of foreclosure the second mortgage is wiped out. For this reason second mortgage-holders often bid in on properties at foreclosure sales, since buying the property, paying off the first mortgage, and reselling it is the only way they can recover their investment. Often banks that grant only first mortgages will have friendly agreements with other lending agencies in which the banks promise not to bid against second mortgage-holders in foreclosures, providing the banks' own interests are protected. Thus in a foreclosure in which the first mortgage is $8,000 and the second $2,000, the second mortgage-holder might open the bidding at $10,000, then rebid against any competition up to the market value of the property. If that happened to be only $10,000, the opening bid could be the only one. In such an instance, after the first mortgage-holder received his $8,000, the new owner would sell the property for $10,000, making no profit but getting back the $2,000 he loaned as a second mortgage. The higher risk of losing the investment is the reason the interest rate on second mortgages is higher.

Another form of lien is what in some states is called a *security agreement,* in others a *chattel mortgage.* In law a chattel is any item of personal property. A chattel mortgage or a security agreement is therefore a lien against personal property. When you arrange to buy a car on time, the balance you owe constitutes the chattel mortgage against your car.

This type of lien is used in other instances than simply buying on time. When you borrow from a loan company, you may be required to give a lien against your household furniture as security for the loan. When you borrow from a pawnbroker, you grant a lien against the item you leave as security. In many states the law places an automatic lien against personal property when the owner contracts to have some service performed in connection with it. If you allow a TV repairman to take your set into his shop for repair, then refuse to pay the bill, the repairman may legally hold your set until the bill is paid, because he has a lien against it for the amount of the bill. Likewise if you hire a moving company to move your furniture, then refuse to pay when the truck arrives at your new home, the company is not only legally entitled to hold your furniture until you do pay but also may charge an additional amount for storage until the lien is satisfied.

In the last two cases the law gives the holder of the lien the right to sell the property in order to satisfy the lien without having to obtain court permission if payment is not made within a specified time. Pawned items may similarly be sold without court permission if they are not reclaimed. These are exceptions granted by special legislation in order to relieve the businesses involved of the expense of going to court in common and recurring situations.

ACTIONS TO OBTAIN COMPENSATION FOR WRONGS

These are the oldest of all legal actions. We have already covered their historical development in some detail in Chapter 1. In modern courts all such actions are based on the premise that wronged persons are entitled to monetary compensation from the wrong-doer.

A wrong does not necessarily have to be to person or property. It may be to the injured party's reputation, in which case the defendant may be sued for *defamation of character*. It may be only to his pocketbook, or it may even be only to his convenience.

In the latter two cases the most common circumstance giving rise to a claim would be failure or refusal to meet the terms of a contract. For instance, a road-building contractor would have grounds to ask for compensation for his financial loss from a cement manufacturer who failed to deliver a carload of cement by a specified date, resulting in the contractor having to pay workers for standing around idle. A homeowner could ask for compensation for the inconvenience suffered because a moving company delivered his furniture a month later than the agreed-upon delivery date.

The possible grounds for claiming compensable damage are endless. They range all the way from the actual case of a movie director suing a TV station for damage to his artistic reputation because the film was cut to make room for commercials, thereby, according to him, destroying the story line, to the actual case of a man suing his dentist for installing a filling that acted as a crystal radio set. The filling picked up a local radio station, forcing the plaintiff to hear its broadcast around the clock and nearly driving him crazy. By far the most common type of compensation case is for personal injury, which is covered in detail in Chapter 6. The award in a compensation case is in the form of a money judgment identical to those granted in debt cases and is usually enforceable by the same kind of procedures—that is, by *execution,* or a direction to the sheriff to take the necessary steps to collect the judgment.

ACTIONS TO END EXISTING WRONGS

In cases where a continuing wrong is going on, the court may order such a wrong to end. Often such an order is accompanied by a simultaneous order to pay compensation for the amount of wrong already done, but as money judgments have already been covered, we will consider only the termination-of-wrong phase of such actions. Probably the most common type of such cases to come before the courts is wrongful possession of property. It should be understood that wrongful possession does not necessarily mean criminal possession nor even necessarily illegal possession. If someone moves into a vacant house you own without your permission, it is not necessary to bring civil suit to get him out; you may merely have him arrested for trespassing. Similarly, if someone steals your car, it will automatically be returned to you by the police if they can find it, and the only court action taken against the thief will be criminal action. Wrongful possession therefore merely means that the person in possession of the property is not legally entitled to it, not necessarily that he obtained such possession by criminal means.

If the case involves real property, it is called an *action in ejectment.* The 1969 municipal court case of *Winton v. Lehman* in Los Angeles is as good an example as any of this type of action. Thomas Winton, an apartment-house owner, attempted to evict tenant Julius Lehman in order to move a Winton relative into

Lehman's apartment, but there was a written lease with some time yet to run. Lehman was not behind in his rent, had properly maintained the premises, and other tenants had no complaints about him. He claimed that under the terms of the lease he could be evicted only for such causes.

There was a clause in the lease stating that the tenant had to vacate the premises if the landlord decided to make personal use of them, however. The court had to decide if this meant, as Lehman claimed, only if the landlord himself wanted to move in or, as Winton claimed, if it included moving in a member of his family whom he did not intend to charge rent. In this case the court sided with the landlord, and the tenant had to get out.

If the case involves personal property, it is called an *action in replevin.* An example would be when a rooming-house landlady refuses to surrender the trunk of an ex-roomer until she is paid for damages she claims he did to his room. In some states such seizure would be legal if *rent* was owed, but in most states the courts would rule against the landlady in this instance. The court would hold that her proper remedy would be to bring action for a monetary judgment to cover the damages, but that she had no right to try to enforce such payment on her own by seizing the defendant's property.

Sometimes after a judgment awards a plaintiff possession of some item of property, the item cannot be located. The plaintiff must then go back to court and ask for money compensation in lieu of the property. In many cases the plaintiff will be aware in advance that the property in question will be difficult to locate. He may even have reason to believe that the defendant is deliberately concealing it. He therefore may ask the court to order that if the property cannot be found, the value of the item must be paid him in money.

This is not always easy for the court. If the property in question is something like a motorboat, it is simple enough for the judge to find out what it would cost to buy an item of equivalent value and to fix the money judgment accordingly, but let's say the item is an original portrait in oil of the plaintiff's grandmother. The judge or jury is confronted with the problem of fixing a precise monetary value on an item the plaintiff may claim is an artistic masterpiece, the defendant may claim is a worthless daub, and in either event is irreplaceable. As in the case of the county judge who had to determine the goodwill value of a sign, such a figure must literally be picked out of the air.

Except for money judgments in unsecured debts, judgments in the three major classes of actions we have so far considered are usually *in rem,* which means against the property, rather than *in personam,* or against the person. That is, the court merely decides whether or not the money should be paid or the property should be surrendered and fixes no penalty for noncompliance with the judgment. Instead the court makes available to the winner of the lawsuit whatever legal apparatus there is to enforce compliance. Thus, if the loser of a damage suit fails to pay the judgment ordered, he cannot be held in contempt of court, but the victor may garnish the loser's wages or have some property he owns executed upon and sold at public auction in order to satisfy the debt. Also, in a property judgment, if the loser refuses to turn over the property decreed to belong to the victor, the latter can have it forcibly seized by the sheriff or other officer of the court.

There are some exceptions to this general rule. For instance, in an action of replevin in which the court has reason to believe the defendant is deliberately concealing the property in question, instead of merely fixing an alternate money judgment in case the property cannot be located, the judge may make the order to turn over the property a judgment *in personam.* Now, if the property is not produced, the defendant may be held in contempt of court and be fined and/or imprisoned. This is not common, however, for a plaintiff usually asks for such a judgment only if the item in question is unique and irreplaceable, such as the above-mentioned oil portrait.

PROCEDURES TO ENFORCE MONEY JUDGMENTS

When a court hands down a money judgment, a document describing the judgment is attached to the case file and becomes a permanent record of the court. This document does not order the debtor to pay the amount but merely declares that it is due. (In actual practice the judgment is sometimes worded as an order to pay, but since the court granting the judgment has no authority to enforce such an order by contempt proceedings, the judgment is still merely a declaration that the amount is due, regardless of its wording.) It also implies, and in some jurisdictions specifically states, that the creditor is entitled to the services of the sheriff, marshal, or other appropriate officer of the court in enforcing collection. The failure to pay, or even the refusal to pay, does not subject the debtor to any criminal penalties, therefore. It merely makes him liable to further civil action by the plaintiff.

If the debtor pays the judgment, in most states the creditor must furnish him with a document acknowledging not only receipt of the money but also specifically stating that the payment has satisfied the judgment. This is called a *satisfaction* in some states, a *satisfaction piece* in others. The debtor files this with the clerk of the court that handed down the judgment, and the clerk attaches it to the case record. If any future dispute about the judgment then arises, the complete record may be found in the court files.

If the debtor fails to pay the judgment, the creditor may take any of a number of alternate actions. One of the most common is to record the judgment with the county recorder as a lien against real estate owned by the debtor. When such a lien is recorded, it applies against any and all real estate owned by the debtor and, in most states, against any such property acquired by him within a specified number of years. Such a lien, of course, applies only against the equity the debtor has in the property and can be satisfied only after other liens already recorded against it have been taken care of.

As often as not the creditor takes no other action after filing such a lien, merely allowing it to hang over the debtor's head as a threat to force him to pay the judgment, but if payment is not forthcoming within a reasonable length of time, the creditor may force the sale of the property in order to collect. The procedure to do this is for the creditor's lawyer to draw up an order called an *execution against property* and send it to the clerk of the court that issued the judgment. This order is directed to the appropriate court officer, such as the sheriff or marshal, who is responsible for enforcing the collection of judgments. If the order is in proper form, the court clerk will issue it.

The officer served with this order is required to levy execution on the property and sell it at public auction. In all states there are certain *homestead exemptions* not subject to such liens, however. In some states the home the debtor lives in is totally exempt, regardless of its value; in others the exemption is limited to a specific sum. Any competent lawyer would be aware in advance of such restrictions, though, and would not be likely to draw up an execution against property that could not be fulfilled.

Liens may also be filed against personal property to satisfy money judgments, but here again there are statutory limits. Most states exempt from attachment all tools used in debtor's trade—such as the truck, ladders, saws, and clippers of a tree surgeon, for instance—and certain other items such as household furnishings. It should be noted that such exemption is only for liens to collect money judgments, however. If you have signed a chattel mortgage or security agreement against such property to obtain a loan, that is an entirely different matter.

Also within certain statutory limits a lien may be filed against a debtor's bank account to satisfy a money judgment. In some states a certain minimum balance is exempt. In most, under certain circumstances the bank is allowed to apply whatever money is in the account against whatever unsecured notes the debtor owes the bank before releasing the balance, if any. One circumstance is if the note or notes are overdue, even by one day. Another is when the borrower has filed a financial statement with the bank describing his complete financial situation. Nearly all banks require such a statement before they will grant an unsecured loan—a loan granted on signature only, with nothing put up for security. In the small print in such statements there is customarily a clause stating that all of the obligations to the bank shall immediately become due and payable, without demand or notice, if a writ of attachment, garnishment, execution, or other legal process is issued against the account of the signer.

Assume someone obtains a money judgment against you for $900. You have a $1,000 savings account in a California bank, where there is no minimum balance exempt from levy. The judgment creditor slaps a lien against it for $900, but the bank is also carrying a personal note on you for $500, and you filed a financial statement in order to obtain the note. The bank will close out your account, pay off the note, and turn the $500 balance over to your judgment creditor. It should be noted that the bank may use this procedure only when the note is unsecured. This is because it has the option of attaching the property put up for security if a levy against a borrower's bank account leaves him unable to pay a secured note.

When there is no real or personal property available to satisfy a judgment, or it is unfeasible to file a lien against such property, *garnishment proceedings* may be instituted against the debtor's income from different sources. The court issues this order not to the debtor but to the person who is the source of the income. Usually this is the debtor's employer, but it may be the administrator of a trust fund, a company paying royalties on a patent, or any other source.

The *garnishee,* as the person to whom such a court order is directed is called, is required to withhold a certain portion of the money due the debtor and pay it to the creditor instead (or sometimes to an officer of the court, who relays it to the creditor). Recent federal legislation standardized the procedure for garnishment throughout the country, except for the percentage of wages subject to garnishment. The act permits that percentage to remain subject to state law, which varies from state to state but in no case allows more than 50 percent of income to be seized in this manner. In general the federal act is designed to end unfair tactics against the debtor, such as the previous right of a creditor in many states to institute garnishment proceedings without the debtor first being granted a hearing.

In cases where a debtor neither owns property nor has income from a specific source (as a handyman who does odd jobs for a constantly changing clientele of homeowners) some states permit the creditor to ask the court to order the debtor to pay a certain amount weekly or monthly until the judgment is satisfied. When such an order is issued, it is *in personam,* and failure to pay places the debtor in contempt of court. Usually such an order requires payment to be made to an officer of the court rather than directly to the creditor so that the court can immediately know if the order is not being complied with. This procedure also protects the debtor from the possibility of the creditor's falsely claiming he never received a payment.

Chapter 5

ACTIONS IN EQUITY

INJUNCTIONS

An injunction is a court order enjoining a wrongdoer to desist from performing or continuing some practice harmful to the plaintiff. What it amounts to is an official notice by the court that if the practice is not stopped, the defendant may be fined and/or imprisoned for contempt of court. Most injunctions order the wrongdoer to stop some practice he is carrying on, but sometimes an injunction is obtained to prevent the defendant from carrying out an action he is merely contemplating. The example given in Chapter 2, concerning the neighbor whose contemplated drainage ditch might undermine a dividing wall, falls into this category.

Injunctions of this type are less common primarily because it is more difficult to obtain them. Before a court will issue an injunction, it is necessary for the plaintiff to establish to the judge's satisfaction that the practice he wishes enjoined is harmful to him. Obviously this is easier in a case where the objectionable practice is already going on. For instance, a farmer whose land is downstream of a paper mill that is polluting a stream that runs through his property can have the water analyzed and bring into court actual scientific evidence of the damage done to the stream, but if someone is merely contemplating building a paper mill upstream of him, proving potential damage will be considerably more difficult.

Until the court of chancery developed in England, monetary judgments and orders to return property to its rightful owners were the only remedies offered by the courts. Even after this special court came into being, it was available only after the search for redress in the regular courts had been exhausted, and even in the court of chancery the injunction was used only as a last resort. This principle still obtains in United States courts. In all states and in the federal courts an injunction is regarded as a sort of last-ditch measure when there is no other adequate legal remedy. The injury or threatened injury must, at least in theory, be irreparable merely through awarding damages or granting possession of property.

This does not mean other legal remedies must necessarily be tried before a request for an injunction can be made. There are obvious situations in which the only appropriate action is to ask for an injunction. All that is required is that the situation be such that it is clear to the court that other types of action would not afford the plaintiff relief. For instance, if an ex-husband continues to harass his divorced wife by phoning her or accosting her in public, she is not required to bring suit for damages against him before asking for an injunction to make him stop bothering her. Her first and only legal action may be to request an injunction.

A common type of injunction is that in which a business is ordered to stop using the name or symbol of some organization that has public respect, thus creating the false impression that the organization either manufactures the product distributed by the business or sponsors it. Since its inception in 1881 the American National Red Cross has been forced to ask the courts for dozens of injunctions forbidding manufacturers to use the name Red Cross for everything from Red Cross liver pills to Red Cross cigarettes. The Y.M.C.A., the Boy Scouts of America, the Girl Scouts, and virtually every other non-profit organization enjoying widespread respect has had the same problem.

The courts have consistently granted such injunctions when it was clear that the intent was merely to cash in on the organization's good name. When commercial use of the name or symbol preceded its use by the organization, however, the courts have just as consistently held that the business had as much right to the use of the name as the organization. Thus you will still find Red Cross shoes on the market, because the shoe company is older than the American National Red Cross. A manufacturer may similarly ask for an injunction against a competitor who starts distributing a product with a name too close to his own. If you started manufacturing and distributing a soft drink called Seven-Upp, you could anticipate an injunction ordering you to rename it.

There are some situations in which injunctions are specifically provided for by statute. Federal law, for instance, provides for automatic injunctions against those proved guilty of patent or copyright infringement. Antitrust laws expressly authorize injunctions in cases of restraint of interstate or foreign trade. The Labor-Management Act of 1947 (usually called the Taft-Hartley Act) provides for injunctions against unions to stop strikes and boycotts which either threaten the safety of the nation or constitute unfair labor practices.

An example of the former might be a strike paralyzing the railroads. Unfair labor practices, as enumerated in the Taft-Hartley Act, include such things as a strike or a boycott to force an employer or a self-employed person to join a union or to force an employer to recognize a labor organization that has not been certified by the National Labor Relations Board. The N.L.R.B. is an independent agency of the United States government consisting of five members and a general counsel appointed by the President with the consent of the Senate. Its function is to supervise labor-management relations and to prevent specified unfair labor practices by both employers and unions. Its method of stopping a strike or a boycott is for the general counsel to petition a United States district court for an injunction or temporary restraining order.

The latter is the most common first maneuver on the part of the N.L.R.B. A temporary restraining order merely enjoins the party being restrained to suspend the practice objected to by the plaintiff until the court can hold a hearing on whether or not an injunction should be issued. The order may be issued *ex parte,* which means the party being restrained need not be present nor even have been informed of the contemplated petition. The defendant must, of course, be notified of the hearing on the injunction, however, and be given an opportunity to contest it.

DIRECTORY JUDGMENTS

The directory judgment might be called the reverse of the injunction in that it is a court order requiring the defendant to perform some act rather than calling upon him to cease some practice. Such orders are not as common as injunctions, because in general the courts feel that the ordinary course of asking for damages best serves the cause of justice when a defendant has failed to keep an agreement. If a painter signed a contract to paint your house, then refused to do the job, few if any judges would grant you a *decree of specific performance of contract* ordering him to do the job. Instead the court would suggest you sue him for damages and hire another painter. Personal-services contracts are generally not enforceable by such a decree because public policy is against "involuntary servitude."

There are instances when forcing compliance is obviously the most equitable remedy, however. *Fitzer v. Turner,* tried in Department 98 of the Los Angeles superior court, is a good example. In August, 1969, John Turner signed an agreement to sell his downtown Los Angeles dry-cleaning establishment to Harold Fitzer. The deal included deed to the property in which the business was housed, all the dry-cleaning and pressing equipment, a delivery truck, the business records, and the right to continue to use the business name.

On a transfer of real property the matter generally has to go through *escrow*. Escrow is the delivery of property conditionally to a third person, not the owner, who holds it until certain conditions have been met, then delivers it to the new owner. Usually the escrow agent is the bank of the savings and loan association that holds the mortgage. The purchaser puts up the purchase price (actually, in most cases, he merely puts up the agreed-upon down payment, and the lending agency puts up the rest), and the seller puts up the deed to the property. Both are held by the escrow agent until the title has been searched to make sure the seller has the right to dispose of the property. When all necessary conditions have been met, title to the property is turned over to the purchaser and the money is turned over to the seller.

After the sale of the dry-cleaning establishment had gone through escrow, Turner decided to back out and refused to vacate the premises. Instead he offered Fitzer his money back, plus a small additional amount for his inconvenience. Fitzer asked the superior court for a decree of specific performance of contract.

The court could have told Fitzer to sue for damages, then go buy some other cleaning establishment, but the situation here was not as simple as that of the house painter mentioned above. Any number of competent painters could be presumed to be available to the homeowner. There was no equivalent number of cleaning establishments available for Fitzer to purchase, though, and even if there had been, none could be in the unique location this one was or have the precise facilities and business advantages. The court therefore ordered Turner to fulfill the contract.

Like the injunction, the federal government has come to use the directory judgment to some extent. In antitrust actions it frequently obtains decrees ordering corporations to divest themselves of certain subsidiaries or even to break up their corporations into two or more separate companies in order to end monopolies.

Another common form of this type of order is the *writ of mandamus*. Typically such a writ would be issued by a court, on the request of a stockholder, to force a company or corporation official to perform some act required either by statute or by the company bylaws. For example, if a corporation president neglected to call an annual stockholders' meeting, and such a meeting was required by the corporate bylaws, a writ of mandamus ordering him to call the meeting might be issued. This type of writ may also be issued against a public official, at the instigation of a taxpayer, to force him to perform a mandatory duty. A city comptroller who refused public access to his books when the city charter provided that any taxpayer had the right to examine such books could be forced to produce them by a writ of mandamus.

DECLARATORY JUDGMENTS

In 1921 New York State enacted a statute permitting *declaratory judgments* to be handed down. Prior to this, when a person was uncertain as to just what his legal rights were in a given situation, the only way to find out was to perform some deliberate act that would get him haled into court in order to make a test case out of it. Assume, for example, that a tenant believed but was not sure that under the terms of his lease he was entitled to hold back his rent until the landlord made certain repairs. The only way he could find out was not to pay the rent and have the landlord drag him into court, because courts were empowered to act only in cases in which one of the parties claimed damage. The New York State law permitted litigants to ask for judgments defining the rights of the different parties to contracts and agreements, even when there was no claim for damages or other relief. In 1934 Congress enacted a law permitting the federal courts to issue declaratory judgments. Since then most states have enacted similar laws, so that the decree is now available in courts throughout the country.

CUSTODY ACTIONS

When couples applying for legal separation or divorce have minor children, custody is always one of the factors considered by the court. There are also many cases of separation without court action in which the parents have merely reached personal agreement about where the children will live. There are other cases in which one parent or the other has simply assumed custody over the other's objection. Still others include a third party, such as a grandparent, who has actual custody. In all these cases there are the seeds for custody battles. There are also often cases in which both parents are either dead or have disappeared, and two or more relatives are fighting over custody of the children. Such actions may be begun as *habeas corpus* proceedings. *Habeas corpus* is a Latin phrase whose literal meaning is "you should have the body"—"body" not meaning a corpse in this case but a person in custody. In both English and United States law it is a writ issued by a court commanding a person having custody of another to produce the detained person for the purpose of determining the legality of the custody.

More commonly the petitioner may simply ask the court for a custody hearing. The court will then order the children to be brought before the court pending a decision under *substantive law* as to who will have custody. Substantive law is law that regulates rights, as opposed to *adjective law,* which prescribes remedies and procedures for enforcing rights. In all states the courts base their decisions primarily on the welfare of the children and are not required to follow any agreements previously made by the litigants. The principle here is that children are in no sense property, and therefore contractual agreements concerning their "ownership" have no legal validity.

INHERITANCE PROCEEDINGS

Probate or surrogate courts are primarily concerned with the disposition of the estates of deceased persons. They interpret the meanings of wills and supervise the management and distribution of estates by the executors named in such wills. When persons die intestate (without having made wills) or their wills fail to name executors, the court appoints an administrator to perform the same function. In some states such courts have the additional responsibility of hearing adoption proceedings and administering the estates of incompetent persons and infants.

The bequeathing of estates by will is a relatively recent development in law, considering the thousands of years our legal system has been evolving. As was pointed out in Chapter 2, in primitive societies there was no recognition of real property rights, so estates consisted of nothing but personal property. Through the period of barbarism such personal property usually comprised tools, weapons, and livestock for the most part, and custom decreed exactly how it should be distributed.

Tools and weapons commonly went to the eldest son or to the nearest male relative if there were no sons. Among the Germanic tribes livestock was usually divided equally among all children, including daughters. Among the Asiatic tribes the division was usually among only sons, as women had no inheritance rights. Custom required male relatives to provide for their women, though. Thus if a man without children died and his closest male relative was a brother, his widow would inherit nothing and his whole estate would go to the brother; however, the brother would be morally obligated to take care of the widow so that her economic situation would remain about the same as it was as a wife. Among the tribes of both Europe and Asia property descended to heirs by fixed custom, requiring neither wills nor court intervention.

When ownership of real property began to be recognized, the traditional rules governing the inheritance of personal property at first carried over to it too, but very quickly laws providing for its disposition to heirs began to be passed. By the time of the Middle Ages the laws of inheritance were quite explicit. In general the eldest son, with rare exceptions, was the sole heir of real property, and the law even governed the disposition of most personal property. So wills were still not only unnecessary but also had no legal validity. Inheritance as a matter of legal right prevailed over the desires of the individual as to how his estate was to be distributed after his death.

In England the descent of real property was regulated by law until the sixteenth century. By then there had developed the right to bequeath personal property by will, but even this right was limited. For instance, a certain portion of every estate, by ecclesiastical law, automatically went to the church. To make sure that the church got its share, the ecclesiastical courts had become the traditional administrators of the personal-property portions of all decedents' estates. The result was that over the years a considerable body of ecclesiastical law developed regulating the distribution of personal property of people who died intestate.

When, during the sixteenth century, English law began to recognize the right to will real property to whomever the owner pleased, it was only natural that the ecclesiastical courts, already the recognized tribunals for probate matters, should assume jurisdiction over all inheritance proceedings. By allowing this, the Crown was not really surrendering any jurisdiction to the church, however. In 1532, two years before his final break with the papacy, Henry VIII had compelled the English clergy to acknowledge him instead of the Archbishop of Canterbury as the head of the English church. In effect this made the ecclesiastical courts crown courts, in that they were now directly responsible to the king.

This was still the situation in England when the first English colonies were established in America. The colonists brought no ecclesiastical courts with them, but they did bring English law. The result was a classic case of compromising with tradition when circumstances make it impossible to comply with it strictly. The colonial governor, as deputy of the Crown, was deemed to be also the king's representative as head of the Church of England. In a number of colonies, New York being one, the governor decided this gave him authority to administer probate matters and established a tribunal separate from the regular courts to handle such business.

These tribunals in some cases survived after the American Revolution to form the separate probate courts that exist in many states today. The existence of these courts stems more from this historical chain of events than from any practical reason for separating probate actions from other matters of law and equity. There really is no practical reason why the administration of wills cannot be handled by the regular civil courts.

As a matter of fact, in a number of states the so-called probate court is actually not a court at all. It is merely an administrative office where the papers necessary to processing wills are registered and which has the power of affirming only uncontested wills. Any questions requiring judical determination have to be referred to the regular courts.

ACTIONS TO END MARRIAGES

Under the law marriage is a legal contract. Unless there is some dispute over the terms of the dissolution, however, most contracts may be terminated by mutual consent without the necessity of court action. This is not the case with marriage. It is nearly unique in that it *always* requires a judicial decree to end the contract. (It is not wholly unique because adoption contracts also require judicial action to be terminated.) A marriage contract may be terminated by divorce or annulment, or it may merely be suspended by separation. We will consider the last first.

There are many cases of separation in which the spouses merely move apart without bothering to go through any legal maneuvers. Even though they may not have contact for years, the marriage still remains in full force in such cases, and both parties still have the same legal responsibilities to each other that marriage involves. The husband, for instance, remains responsible for his wife's debts in the event she decides to run up a lot of bills at department stores.

Such responsibilities can be limited if the spouses obtain judicial sanction to separate. The *separation agreement* is a voluntary arrangement agreed to by both parties in which the husband and wife ask court permission to live apart and which defines the future responsibilities of both in such matters as the support and custody of children and the support of the wife. Such an agreement, once approved by the court, relieves both parties of the normal responsibilities of marriage other than those specified in the separation agreement.

When only one party wants separation, or the terms of separation cannot be agreed upon, the court may be asked to issue an order granting legal separation and stipulating its terms. Depending on the state, this is called a *decree of legal separation,* a *judicial separation, separate maintenance,* or a *limited divorce.* Whatever its official terminology, what it amounts to is a decree permitting the marriage partners to live apart without risking the charge of desertion, limiting their future responsibilities to each other to the terms fixed by the court, but not allowing them to remarry.

Divorce, in some states called *absolute divorce* in order to distinguish it from limited divorce and in a few states now called *dissolution of marriage,* completely ends the marriage contract, but it also fixes the future responsibilities of the parties to each other in the same manner that a separation decree does. Customarily the decree includes how property is to be divided, includes alimony (called spouse support in some states), fixes child support, grants the custody of children, and stipulates what the visiting rights are of the person not granted custody. The divorce laws of the fifty states vary tremendously in the grounds on which divorce may be obtained, on the length of time one must be a resident of the state before filing for divorce, and on the length of time divorced persons must wait after the decree is issued before it is legal to remarry. This last is called the *interlocutory period,* and as an example of how much it varies, in New York State it is one year, in California six months, and in Missouri only one day.

The thing that keeps this situation from becoming a complete shambles is the Constitutional stipulation that the various states must give "full faith and credit" to the laws of other states. Thus, in most cases, the State of Maryland, for instance, must recognize divorces granted in Nevada, Mississippi, or any other state. This does not mean that every state must automatically accept unquestionably the divorce decrees granted by other states, and they frequently are contested. Such decrees do automatically stand if neither party to the divorce contests them, of course, as the trial courts have sufficient business to occupy them without going out of their ways to examine the legality of decrees no one is disputing, but numerous divorce cases contested by one party or the other have gone all the way to the Supreme Court.

Most such cases have been contested on the grounds that the court granting the decree lacked proper jurisdiction because the plaintiff was not a bona fide resident of the state. In 1944 the Supreme Court held that it was necessary for a person to establish residence "in good faith" in a state other than the one where he had been living in order to obtain a valid divorce there. This would seem to have been a blow to the Nevada divorce mills, where anyone could obtain a divorce after six weeks' residence, but the Nevada lawyers merely added another question to the routine ones they asked their clients on the stand:

> LAWYER: When you moved to Nevada, was your intention to become a permanent resident, and is that still your intention?
> PLAINTIFF: Yes.

Presumably this constituted good faith. If the plaintiff changed his or her mind immediately after the decree was handed down and caught the next plane back to the former state of residence, that was no business of the court.

The possibility of injustice is obvious when one spouse can travel to another state to get a divorce, sometimes without the defendant having a proper chance to contest the action. The Supreme Court has ruled on this matter several times, most notably in the 1957 decision in *Vanderbilt v. Vanderbilt*. When they separated in 1952, the Vanderbilts were residents of California. In 1953 the husband obtained a Nevada divorce. Meantime the wife had moved to New York State, was never served papers from the Nevada court, and did not appear before the court. Subsequent to the Nevada decree the wife filed suit for alimony in the New York State supreme court. The court recognized the Nevada decree as valid insofar as dissolving the marriage was concerned but held that the Nevada court had no personal jurisdiction over the wife and no power to extinguish her rights under New York State law to financial support from her ex-husband. Therefore, although the Nevada decree granted no alimony, the New York court declared its right to direct the ex-husband to make support payments and ordered such payments. The United States Supreme Court upheld the New York State court's reasoning.

Grounds for divorce vary tremendously from state to state. Until the recent liberation of its divorce laws, New York State was the most restrictive, permitting divorce for adultery only, but divorce may now be obtained there for a number of reasons. Grounds now include abandonment for two years, mental or physical cruelty, insanity after five years of confinement to a mental hospital, prison confinement after three years, and living apart for two years under a decree of separation or a properly filed separation agreement.

In Missouri divorce grounds include pregnancy at the time of the marriage, impotence at the time of the marriage, desertion for one year, nonsupport, treatment cruel and barbarous enough to endanger life, habitual drunkenness for one year, a felony conviction even without imprisonment, life imprisonment, fraud, an existing prior marriage (in most states this is grounds for annulment but not for divorce), personal indignities, and vagrancy of the husband. In California a new law went into effect in 1970 that was unique not only in the United States but also in the whole Western world. Since then Iowa and Texas have passed similar legislation, and New York State is studying the approach. Because these laws are so different from those in the other forty-seven states, we will table them for the moment and come back to them later.

Adultery is grounds for divorce in all forty-seven states aside from California, Iowa, and Texas. Unchastity at the time of marriage is grounds in the six states of Idaho, Kansas, Kentucky, Michigan, Utah, and Virginia. Sterility is grounds in Mississippi and Utah.

Being underage at the time of marriage is grounds for divorce in Connecticut, Delaware, Rhode Island, and Washington. In Florida, Georgia, Maryland, Mississippi, Pennsylvania, and Rhode Island divorce may be obtained if your spouse is a relative to whom marriage is prohibited by law. In only six states—Arizona, Georgia, Kentucky, Pennsylvania, Rhode Island, and Washington—can divorce be obtained by the victim of a shotgun marriage on the grounds of force or duress; however, this is grounds for annulment in the other states. Other grounds for divorce allowed in some states include drug addiction, incompatibility, membership in a religious sect that does not believe in marriage, loathsome disease, unnatural behavior, and in twelve states, even a violent and ungovernable temper.

As can be seen, divorce laws vary too much from state to state to make very many generalizations, but the systems in all states other than California, Iowa, and Texas have one thing in common: Fault must be shown before a divorce may be granted. The plaintiff must always be the innocent victim of wrongful acts by the defendant. Two people cannot simply walk into court and tell the judge they are fed up with each other and want out. One must always be the villain.

Oddly, when there is a counter suit in which the defendant submits evidence that the plaintiff has also committed an act that is grounds for divorce, the court will sometimes deny divorce to either. The judicial thinking here seems to be that if both parties are bad marriage partners, they deserve each other and should be forced to continue to put up with each other. One result of the law's insistence that fault be shown has been for the divorce courts to be flooded with trumped-up evidence. Many, possibly even most, divorces are actually by mutual agreement, but because blame must be shown, it is common for the defendant, usually the husband, to furnish evidence deliberately.

As adultery is grounds for divorce in every state except the three with new laws, one of the most common devices is for the husband either to hire a woman or to get a woman friend to stage an act. The husband arranges for some friend or relative willing to be party to the conspiracy to call at his residence at a specific time. A bedroom door is conveniently left ajar so that the visitor can see a woman lying in bed. Later, at the divorce trial, the witness will testify that on such-and-such a date he visited the defendant's home and saw a strange woman in his bed. Usually he will state that he did not recognize the woman and therefore cannot give her name, but as he is well acquainted with the defendant's wife, he knows it was not she. In such cases everyone concerned—both lawyers, the judge, even the spectators—must at least suspect that there has been collusion, which is against the law in all states. Yet the evidence is accepted without question simply because few divorces could ever be granted if the courts insisted on sticking to the letter of the law.

In 1970 California solved this problem. Since January of that year the term "divorce" is no longer used. The sole grounds for *dissolution of marriage* are now "irreconcilable differences," which attaches blame to neither party. It is an enlightened step away from the general tendency to let divorce trials develop into name-calling battles that leave scars on both sides. As has been mentioned, two other states have so far followed California's lead. Hopefully the other forty-seven will eventually do the same.

An *annulment* is a judicial decree holding that the marriage was illegal from the beginning. Grounds for annulment vary as widely from state to state as do grounds for divorce, but it differs from divorce in that the cause must have existed at the time of the marriage. In most states annulment must be requested as soon as the grounds become known to the wronged party. Assume, for example, that two years after marriage a husband discovers his wife as a teen-ager had a baby and gave it up for adoption. If concealment of such a matter constitutes grounds for annulment in the state they reside in, he must file for it as soon as he learns about it. He cannot wait a few years, perhaps letting the threat of annulment hang over his wife's head constantly, then finally decide he wants the marriage annulled. Continuing to live with his wife for even a short period—in some cases for even one day—is construed by the courts as evidence of forgiveness and forever nullifies the wrong as grounds for future action.

In some states it is easier to get an annulment than a divorce when no children are involved. The courts in general are reluctant to grant annulments when there are children, since the legal effect is to declare the children illegitimate: For childless couples, particularly if they are young, however, the law tends to take the benign view that it is best to give them a chance to start life over again without the stigma of being divorced.

As in divorce actions, annulment proceedings are conducive to rigged evidence. Before New York State modernized its divorce laws, there were several grounds for annulment, even though adultery was the only ground for divorce. The result was that most childless couples who decided to split up went that route. I once witnessed an annulment proceeding in New York State in which the evidence presented was virtually unbelievable yet was accepted by the court without comment. The first witness was the plaintiff wife. Her testimony, under questioning by her own lawyer, went something like this:

LAWYER: Before you were married, did you and your husband discuss children?

WITNESS: Yes, we agreed to have two.

LAWYER: Do you have any children?

WITNESS: No, sir.

LAWYER: Why not?

WITNESS: Because he changed his mind and says he no longer wants them. He flatly refuses.

Later the plaintiff's sister was called as a witness. She testified that she had been present when the defendant proposed marriage to the plaintiff.

LAWYER: Did you hear any mention of children at that time?

WITNESS: Yes, sir. My sister said she didn't want to get married unless she could have two children. He promised that if she would marry him, she could have two.

Subsequently the sister testified that she had also been present during a more recent conversation between the plaintiff and the defendant when the husband stated that he didn't care what he had promised before marriage; he now wanted no children.

The judge accepted this incredible testimony with a straight face. Annulment was granted on the grounds that the defendant had failed to keep his premarital agreement and therefore had fraudulently induced the plaintiff into marriage. If the judge thought it odd that the defendant had proposed marriage when a witness was so conveniently present, he made no mention of it, nor did he seem to think it strange that the same witness had been conveniently around to overhear the second conversation.

BANKRUPTCY PROCEEDINGS

Prior to 1898 each state had its own laws concerning insolvent debtors. The National Bankruptcy Act passed that year preempted all such state laws. Although the Constitution empowers Congress to establish "uniform laws on the subject of bankruptcies throughout the United States," Congress had previously interpreted this as merely requiring it to insure that state laws had some uniformity. The National Bankruptcy Act took bankruptcy proceedings out of the state courts and threw them into the federal district courts.

About 150,000 personal bankruptcy cases are filed in the United States each year, and there are thousands more cases of business bankruptcy. This huge load has made it impossible for the district courts to administer the Bankruptcy Act without help. The district judges therefore appoint certain lawyers in the various sections of their districts to act as bankruptcy referees. As 90 percent of all debtors who file for personal bankruptcy have no assets whatever to divide among their creditors, there is really no need for a trial, and the referees consequently handle most of the business. The district courts are actually responsible, though, and the more complicated bankruptcy cases are heard there.

When either an individual or a business acquires debts beyond any possibility of paying them off, bankruptcy proceedings may be instituted. In a *voluntary petition of bankruptcy* the debtor asks the court to declare him bankrupt, take over control of his property, sell it off, and prorate the proceeds among his creditors at so much on the dollar. The proceeding may also be initiated by the creditors, in which case it is an *involuntary petition of bankruptcy*. In either event, after the court has doled out to the various creditors whatever assets there are, the debtor is discharged from all further liability to them, with certain exceptions that will be explained later.

When a corporation goes bankrupt, the shareholders are not individually liable for the company's debts; only the assets owned by the company are turned over to the court for distribution among the creditors. Shareholders in certain mutually owned corporations may be held personally liable for corporate debts, but this is too rare a circumstance to merit more than mention. A corporation president can be a multimillionaire, but his personal assets cannot be touched when the business goes bankrupt except when embezzlement or fraud is involved.

When an individual goes bankrupt, it is called *personal bankruptcy*. The most common cause of personal bankruptcy is simply buying too many things on time. A married couple, already paying on a home and a car, will go into debt for a houseful of furniture, a washer and dryer, and a dozen other electrical appliances, all bought on time, then be unable to keep up the payments. The usual pattern is to borrow from a loan company in order to catch up on their delinquent time payments. Since this only adds another monthly time payment that has to be made, their situation is worse when the first loan payment comes due. Often they will go to a second loan company for another loan to get them over that hump and eventually may end up owing as many as a dozen separate loans. Inevitably the point is reached when no more credit is available, creditors can no longer be stood off, and the couple is forced to file a petition of bankruptcy. Regardless of what type of bankruptcy it is, or whether it will be handled by the district court judge or merely referred to a bankruptcy referee, the petition must be filed under oath in a United States district court.

The National Bankruptcy Act sets forth six "acts of bankruptcy" which constitute grounds for filing a petition of bankruptcy against a debtor if he has committed any one of them within four months prior to the filing. These are:

(1) *Fraudulent transfer of property.* If a debtor deeds his house to a relative or transfers possession of other assets to avoid paying his debts, or if he suddenly disappears with a large sum of money, he is guilty of fraudulent transfer. Such transfer is fraudulent only when intent is present, but this is generally inferred from the circumstances.

(2) *Preferential transfer of property.* If a debtor pays off one creditor in full, and the debtor knows that he is insolvent and that the payment will prevent his paying other creditors anything at all or at least less than if he had not paid the one creditor, the debtor is guilty of preferential transfer.

(3) *Permitting a lien on property.* In a sense this is similar to preferential transfer, at least in its effect, in that it gives one creditor an advantage over others, as liens are discharged before the balance of a debtor's assets are divided among his creditors as the result of

bankruptcy. The statute implies that if the debtor knows bankruptcy is going to be inevitable, he should file for voluntary bankruptcy in time to prevent the lien.

(4) *General assignment for the benefit of creditors.* All states except eight—Alaska, Illinois, Maine, Maryland, Nebraska, Oregon, Washington, and Wyoming—allow debtors to make assignments for the benefit of creditors. Under the laws of the other forty-two states a debtor may transfer all his property to an *assignee.* The assignee, who must be bonded, notifies the creditors, usually by publication, of the assignment. When the creditors present their claims, the assignee liquidates the debtor's property and pays as much of the total debt as he can on a prorated basis. Assignment does not extinguish all debts, like bankruptcy, for the unpaid balance is still owed to the creditors. For this reason it is seldom used, but when it is, it constitutes an act of bankruptcy for which a petition of involuntary bankruptcy may be filed.

(5) *Appointment of receiver or trustee.* As receivership is explained a little farther on, it is sufficient here to mention it only as one of the six acts of bankruptcy. It should be noted, though, that only a receivership for the benefit of all creditors constitutes such an act. A *limited receivership,* such as one appointed to manage a specific piece of property pending a mortgage foreclosure, would not constitute an act of bankruptcy.

(6) *Written admission of inability to pay debts.* To constitute an act of bankruptcy under this classification the debtor must admit in writing that he cannot pay his debts and that he is willing to be adjudged a bankrupt. This act of bankruptcy obviously is the one under which voluntary petitions of bankruptcy are

filed. It is possible for this act to be grounds for a petition of involuntary bankruptcy, however. For instance, if the insolvent person makes the admissions outlined in the act in a letter to a business associate, it would constitute an act of bankruptcy.

Just because these six acts of bankruptcy are set forth in the National Bankruptcy Act, it does not follow that a petition of involuntary bankruptcy will automatically be filed by some creditor the moment a debtor commits one of the acts. In receiverships, for instance, it is unlikely such a petition would be filed so long as the receivership is going well, since it was agreed to in advance by the creditors; nor, unless a creditor suspected the debtor was concealing assets, would there be much point in forcing someone into bankruptcy who has made a general assignment for the benefit of creditors. The acts are set forth as grounds for filing a petition if the circumstances warrant it.

In personal bankruptcy, as in money judgments, certain property of the debtor is exempt from attachment. Because the National Bankruptcy Act recognizes the exemptions allowed by the state in which the bankrupt files, these things vary from state to state. In general they are about the same exemptions that are allowed for liens, however. A certain amount of equity in a home used as a residence, all tools used in the debtor's trade or profession, and a certain amount of household goods are exempt. This applies to personal bankruptcy only, of course. When a business goes bankrupt, all assets are attached.

There are some debts that are not discharged by bankruptcy. These still have to be paid by the debtor, even after he goes through bankruptcy, if he subsequently accumulates enough money to pay them. These include debts acquired by fraud, alimony and child support, certain specified money judgments for damages (although most money judgments are wiped out by bankruptcy), and federal, state, county, and municipal taxes.

Insofar as the last item is concerned, nothing, including even death, discharges a federal income-tax liability. It is sometimes reported that the Internal Revenue Service has "settled" for a reduced sum with someone who owes a huge back tax. One of the most highly publicized such cases in recent years was the so-called settlement with former heavyweight champion Joe Louis. In that instance the accrued interest on the tax owed came to more than Louis's annual income. (The government charges 6 percent on unpaid taxes, which means that interest on a million dollars in back taxes amounts to sixty thousand dollars a year.) What the "settlement" amounted to was that after prying out of the former champ every cent the I.R.S. figured it could get, it shelved the debt and stopped demanding that he keep up the interest payments, but if Joe Louis ever discovers a diamond mine in his back yard, a representative of the I.R.S. will be there with his hand out the next day.

Even after his death the I.R.S. will have fourth grab at his estate. First priority is for the costs connected with probate, such as payment of the executor's fee and court costs. Then, because lawyers tend to make our laws, and like all people, they are inclined to look out for their own interests, the law decrees that legal fees are paid out of estates before any other claims are satisfied. Next, because the funeral directors have a powerful lobby, funeral expenses come out of the estate. The Internal Revenue Service gets the fourth bite, then other creditors get theirs, and only then do the heirs get the balance, if any is left.

In the case of business insolvency it is often to the advantage of the creditors to help the business get back on its feet in the hope it will eventually be able to pay off its debts in full instead of settling for part payment by dividing up the assets. When creditors holding two-thirds of the claims against a business and a majority of the shareholders agree that it is worthwhile to try to save the business, the court may place it in *receivership*. For a specified period of time deemed by the court to be adequate to determine if the business will be able to survive under new management, all claims against it are tabled, and the business continues to function under the supervision of the court, run by a court-appointed receiver.

Although companies in receivership are legally under the supervision of the court, the average judge obviously lacks both the time and the specialized knowledge to run the business personally. In practice the way such receiverships work out is that the creditors and the shareholders, and sometimes the company officers, get together and work out a plan of receivership. It may be agreed that one of the creditors will take over the running of the business. If the plan seems workable to the judge, he will approve it and appoint as receiver the person or company recommended. The court thus retains control over the whole situation but makes no attempt to actually run the business.

SPECIAL ACTIONS

There are a few other actions in equity which merit at least mention. Among these are *adjudications of incompetency, dissolutions of partnerships and corpora-*

tions, forfeiture of property used for illegal purposes (such as poachers' traps), *actions for reinstatement* (as employees or organization officers), and *adjudications of labor disputes.* These are such specialized actions that we will merely note them in passing, however, and will not take the time to study them in detail.

Chapter 6

PERSONAL INJURY

More than one hundred thousand persons die every year in the United States from accidents of all types, about half in automobile accidents. Estimates of those accidentally injured seriously enough to require medical attention run as high as ten million. Obviously there are no grounds for damages in large numbers of accidental injuries and deaths. A man who slips in his own bathtub and cracks his head against the faucets might in some remote instance have grounds for suit against the bathtub manufacturer on the grounds that the tub was of unsafe design, but in most such cases the injured person would have difficulty establishing blame against anyone other than himself. There are enough cases in which someone can be held accountable for damages, however, to make personal-injury suits the single most important type of civil litigation. Personal-injury suits of all types account for more than 80 percent of all civil cases filed in the United States and are largely responsible for the congestion in our courts. Roughly a quarter million suits are filed in state courts each year as the result of automobile accidents alone.

For personal-injury suits not involving automobile accidents the same rules apply as for all other civil disputes. Although the trial procedures in personal-injury cases arising out of automobile accidents are no different than in any other personal-injury case, the rules about jurisdiction are sometimes different. When a motor accident involving nonresidents occurs in any state, any criminal charges stemming from the accident have always automatically come under the jurisdiction of the courts in the state where the accident took place. No special legislation was necessary to grant such jurisdiction, because the Constitution gives the states jurisdiction over all criminal acts occurring within their boundaries, except for acts over which the federal government has jurisdiction. Civil actions are another matter, however.

When a resident of New York State, driving his car on a federal highway in Missouri, collides with another car driven by a resident of California, and one or both motorists decides to sue for damages, the question of jurisdiction could get pretty sticky if it depended solely on interpretation of the Constitution. Consequently all fifty states have enacted special legislation giving their own state courts jurisdiction in civil actions arising out of alleged negligent operation of motor vehicles by nonresidents within the states. The justification for assuming such jurisdiction is that the nonresident motorist, the moment he enters the state, gives his implied consent to submit to the state's jurisdiction if he is involved in an accident.

This rule does not abridge the right of a plaintiff to file suit in federal court if the amount of damages claimed exceeds ten thousand dollars, of course. If the proposed judicial reforms detailed in Chapter 8 ever go into effect, however, the rule may apply to *all* automobile accident claims, regardless of amount. Chief Justice Warren E. Burger has said: "In the original concepts of federal jurisdiction an automobile case has no more place in the federal courts than speeding on a city street."

In criminal law a lawyer's ability to negotiate "deals" for his clients for the reduction or the dropping of criminal charges is really more important than his skill in the courtroom, because nine out of ten criminal cases end in such deals instead of going to trial. About the same percentage of personal-injury cases are settled by negotiation before actually coming to trial too, so the civil lawyer's ability to bargain is equally important. In many minor personal-injury cases no suit is ever filed, the lawyer's function being merely to obtain as generous a settlement from an insurance company as he can get by horse-trading with the lawyer for the insurance company, but when the amount of damages asked is large, as a general rule the plaintiff's attorney will take the formal action of drawing up and filing the papers necessary to start suit even if he expects to settle out of court. This is only sound tactics, as it gives him the psychological lever of letting the defense know he is prepared to go to court if no satisfactory settlement is offered.

Just as in criminal cases there are often advantages to both the prosecution and the defense to negotiate a guilty plea in return for a reduced charge, there are similar advantages to both sides in reaching a settlement for personal injuries instead of leaving it up to a jury. The most obvious advantage to the plaintiff is that he gets his award sooner. Two and a half years is the average delay nationwide from the time of filing a damage suit until trial begins. Among major cities Chicago tops the record with an average delay of five years. This gives strong inducement to plaintiffs to accept reasonable settlement offers instead of waiting all that time on the chance that a jury might give more.

The defense, on the other hand, can never be sure that a jury will not give the plaintiff everything he asks for. As an example of how unpredictable juries can be, consider two cases arising out of the same airplane crash a few years back. Since the circumstances surrounding the deaths of all passengers aboard had to be identical, you would think that awards would show some similarity. Nevertheless, for the death of two of the passengers, a young married couple, one jury awarded their four children $775,000. For the death of a single passenger, another jury awarded his widow and twenty-year-old daughter nearly $1,000,000. To make these awards seem even more out of focus, the young couple left no appreciable estate to their children, whereas the single passenger was a multi-millionaire. The highest award ever granted by a jury for personal injury to date was handed down in Reno, Nevada, in 1970. It gave the plaintiff, who had been totally paralyzed in an accident, $3,650,000.

The law has not always been so prone to compensate for personal injury as it is today. Although the principle of compensation goes all the way back to primitive times, the growth of civilization tended to warp the principle. In anthropologically savage and barbaric societies there were no enormous differences in wealth, but the development of civilization brought with it an ever-increasing concentration of wealth in the hands of a few. Since it is only human nature to protect one's own interests, the emerging affluent class very quickly began pushing for laws to protect itself against financial liability for mistreatment of members of the lower classes or for negligence in their dealings with them. Throughout history one of the fundamental purposes of civil law has been to preserve the status quo, or as today's student protesters prefer to put it, to protect the Establishment. For the most part the lawmakers in civilized countries have been major property-owners, with the result that civil law has traditionally been weighted to protect the property and wealth of the haves against encroachment by the have-nots.

Special protection has generally been given to the creators of wealth on the theory that "progress," as exemplified by the growth and expansion of huge industries, is somehow beneficial to all citizens. This philosophy was expressed bluntly and rather tactlessly some years back by President Dwight D. Eisenhower's first Secretary of Defense. Charles E. Wilson, who prior to his cabinet appointment had been president of General Motors Corporation, made the widely publicized remark: "What is good for General Motors is good for the country." Mr. Wilson drew considerable criticism in the press for his unfortunate remark and is still periodically satirized by cartoonist Al Capp in the "L'il Abner" comic strip, where a character named General Bullmoose repeatedly propounds, "What is good for General Bullmoose is good for the country." Despite Charlie Wilson's apologetic "clarifications" of his remark, the probability is that he profoundly believed exactly what he said—and probably a large number of industrial leaders secretly agree with him.

The theory that the creators of wealth merit special immunity to the law has seldom been admitted by legislators, but history is replete with examples indicating that lawmakers have generally thought that way until forced by public outrage to repeal such immunities. For example, in the early days of the Industrial Revolution the law in both England and the United States so heavily favored the employer at the expense of the employee that large numbers of workers in both countries lived virtually as slaves. Workers, even children as young as six, toiled in factories as long as sixteen hours a day for starvation wages, under incredibly miserable conditions. The law not only relieved employers from the responsibilities of paying living wages or providing decent working conditions but even relieved them of responsibility for on-the-job injury to employees.

A number of legal principles established by court decisions in both countries served to entrench this type of favoritism. One of the most outrageous was the principle of *assumption of risk*. Certain hazardous jobs, such as the handling of dynamite, paid premium wages because of the risk involved. Paying such premium wages automatically relieved the employer of responsibility in the event of an accident. It was held that the employee waived all right to damages by accepting the premium wage.

This principle was eventually extended to include virtually all hazardous jobs, whether premium wages were paid or not, when it could be shown that the employee was aware of the hazard when he accepted employment. For instance, it was common knowledge that breathing coal dust over a period of years could cause "black lung" disease. A coal miner therefore had no cause for action if he developed this disease, because he had knowingly assumed the risk of contracting it. He could easily have avoided the risk by finding a less hazardous job, and the coal-mine operator should not be held accountable for the poor judgment of his employees.

One effect of this rule was to leave employers unconcerned about safety measures. Why spend money on improved lighting or for protective shields over dan-

gerous machinery when you were immune to lawsuits?
In its 1893 annual statistical report the United States
Interstate Commerce Commission reported, without
outrage but merely as a matter of general interest, that
accidental deaths among railroad switchmen were so
common that their on-the-job life expectancy was
about seven years, but when, in the 1920's, railroads
began to be held accountable for personal injuries,
suddenly they found money enough to install all sorts
of safety devices. It may be cynically stated as a law
of industrial relations that industry's interest in safe
working conditions increases in direct proportion to its
legal liability for injuries.

Another bonanza for employers at the height of the
Industrial Revolution was the *fellow servant rule*. Under this rule an injury caused by a fellow worker left
no cause for action against the employer. If a construction worker dropped a brick on the head of a
co-worker two floors below, the injured man could recover damages only from the man who dropped the
brick, not from their mutual employer. Since all workers tended to be underpaid, in most cases it was point-
less to attempt to recover even medical expenses from
a co-worker.

The creators of wealth were granted immunity from
damage suits not only from their own employees but
to a large extent from suits brought by consumers as
well. One of the bulwarks of such immunity was the
principle of *privity*, which was defined as "a peculiar
mutual relationship between the .two or more parties
to a transaction." Recovery for damages could not be
made unless privity could be shown. This meant that
a direct relationship between the injured person and
the one who caused the injury had to be shown, or
there was no cause for action.

An example will make this clearer. Jonas Smith bought a shotgun from storekeeper Hiram Jones. The first time Smith fired the shotgun, it exploded, damaging his sight. If Hiram Jones had been a gunsmith and had actually manufactured the gun as well as selling it, Smith could have recovered damages, but because Jones was only a retailer, he could not be held accountable for the malfunction of a weapon he didn't make. At the same time Smith's only direct relationship in the transaction was with the storekeeper, and therefore the manufacturer could not be held accountable either.

Another device, this one primarily designed to protect common carriers from suit, was the advance release of responsibility for any injury incurred by a passenger. (A common carrier is a person or a company that transports persons or goods for hire.) When the railroads were new, it was common practice either to print on the backs of tickets or to post signs next to ticket windows that ticket purchasers waived all right to damages in the event of an accident. The courts repeatedly held that as no one was forced to ride on a train against his will, the purchase of a ticket constituted acceptance of the contract offered by the seller.

This device is still employed by many parking lots whose claim stubs have printed on their backs the statement that customers cannot hold the lot responsible for loss or damage to their cars. Courts no longer recognize such disclaimers, however. Unless the customer actually signs such a waiver, there is no contract and the statement is legally meaningless. Presumably parking-lot proprietors persist in printing it in the hope that some customers will believe it leaves them with

no recourse to recover for damages and won't bother
to consult lawyers.

Still another device to protect the haves from damage suits by the have-nots is the doctrine of *contributory negligence*. For most of the nineteenth century a
plaintiff could recover nothing at all for damages if
the defendant could show that the plaintiff was even
in the slightest degree responsible for his own injuries.
The standard precedent used to support the principle,
both in England and the United States, was a decision
handed down by British Justice Lord Ellenborough in
1809. The case involved a man who had driven his
horse-drawn carriage into a pile of lumber left in the
middle of the road. Lord Ellenborough held that although the defendant was at fault for leaving the lumber in such a dangerous place, the plaintiff could have
avoided running into it if he had been traveling at a
safer speed. The plaintiff was therefore denied all
damages. This case was the most frequently cited
precedent in defense against injury claims both in England and the United States for the next seventy-five
years, but toward the end of the century, courts and
juries began increasingly to reject this particular precedent as too restrictive to serve the cause of justice.

The principle of contributory negligence still exists
in forty-nine of the fifty states. Wisconsin has abolished it and has enacted a statute of *comparative negligence* which provides that accompanying negligence
on the part of a plaintiff shall not bar recovery "if
such negligence was not as great as the negligence of
the person against whom recovery is sought, but any
damages allowed shall be diminished in proportion to
the amount of negligence attributable to the person
recovering." In the other forty-nine states it is no

longer as easy to establish contributory negligence as it was in the nineteenth century. Although the principle remains that recovery is barred if even the slightest degree of negligence on the part of the plaintiff can be shown, neither judges nor juries are inclined to accept as contributory negligence a minor lapse of judgment by the plaintiff when the defendant has been shown to have been grossly negligent.

For instance, let us assume that the defendant, driving drunk, ran past a stop sign at seventy miles an hour and smashed into the plaintiff's car. The plaintiff was sober and was driving with care but was exceeding the thirty-five-mile-an-hour speed limit by five miles an hour. It is extremely unlikely that any jury would accept the defense of contributory negligence, even though, technically, it could.

As another example, assume that the plaintiff sues for damages resulting from an accident under identical circumstances, but this time the defendant produces as a witness a passenger who was riding in the plaintiff's car. The witness testifies that the plaintiff saw that the other car was not going to stop but deliberately made no attempt to brake. The witness states that he knows this, because just before impact the plaintiff said, "That car is going to run the stop sign, but if he hits me, it's his fault." Deliberate failure to avoid an avoidable accident is not only contributory negligence but is also a crime. In this case the plaintiff would be barred from recovery.

In a few states the doctrine of comparative negligence exists alongside the doctrine of contributory negligence but applies only to the amount of damage and not to the cause of the accident. That is, even though the plaintiff may in no way be responsible for the accident's occurrence, the defense may contend that if the plaintiff had not been remiss in some manner, his injury would have been less severe. In these states it is a valid defense in motor-accident cases for the defendant to charge the plaintiff with comparative negligence if the latter was not using a seat belt. In such cases it is not uncommon for the defense to furnish medical testimony by a doctor who, as an expert witness, gives his opinion as to how less severe the injuries would have been if the seat belt had been buckled. It is then up to the jury to assess the difference in terms of dollars and cents.

The labor-union movement has long since forced employers to improve working conditions and to pay decent wages. It has also forced both Congress and the state legislatures to enact laws governing hours and wages, setting safety standards, and providing for compensation for work-connected injuries. Another factor in these reforms, at least insofar as increased wages are concerned, was the rather belated recognition by manufacturers that their employees are all potential customers. Industry as a whole began to realize that you cannot sell luxury items to people living on bare subsistence wages, and that the payment of decent wages was good for the economy in general.

There is a story that the late Walter Reuther, president of the United Auto Workers union, was being shown through the Detroit Ford plant by Henry Ford II. When they came to a new piece of automated equipment designed to replace several men, Ford said, "You won't be able to unionize this, Walter."

Reuther replied, "You won't be able to sell it any cars either, Henry."

For the most part the special immunities granted to

the creators of wealth are now a thing of the past. Society in general has demanded their repeal. The trend can be seen in numerous areas.

Workmen's compensation laws have been a major factor in improving working conditions. Workmen's compensation is actually an insurance program, with the premiums paid for by the employer. The size of each employer's premium increases in direct proportion to the amount paid out in claims to his employees, which has magically inspired a nationwide industrial-safety contest. Many factories now employ full-time safety engineers whose sole function is to maintain a running check on possible safety hazards and correct them before anyone gets hurt.

The consumer no longer buys at his own risk either. Officialdom on all governmental levels has reversed its historical policy toward manufacturers and common carriers, so that the emphasis has now shifted to protection of the general public. The federal government, a number of states, and even some cities now have departments of consumer affairs which keep watchful eyes on what is being offered to the public. The Federal Trade Commission, in the past justly charged with leniency toward industries accused of unfair or deceptive marketing practices, underwent a major personnel shake-up in 1970 and suddenly developed a tough new policy, long overdue. Since then some of the nation's largest corporations have been ordered to halt deceptive advertising practices. Crusading private citizens have done much to protect the interests of the general public too. One of the most conspicuous examples in recent years was a suit for overcharging brought against the General Electric Company on behalf of the plaintiff and several million John Does, the latter, according to the suit, representing all the other customers who had purchased G.E. appliances during the period it was alleged the over-charging took place. When the plaintiff won the suit, the company had to repay millions of dollars to con-sumers who had purchased G.E. appliances during the stipulated period.

One private citizen has made a career of crusading for the protection of the general public against shoddy and unsafe products. Ralph Nader, attorney and au-thor, first attracted national attention with his book *Unsafe at Any Speed,* a scathing criticism of Detroit auto manufacturers' neglect of safety features in their cars. Subsequently he launched crusades against vari-ous other industries and also branched out to expose corruption and inefficiency in state and federal gov-ernmental agencies. A group of similarly dedicated young attorneys have been organized under his direc-tion and are known as Nader's Raiders. Divided into task forces, they travel all over the country delving into matters of interest to the general public and is-suing reports exposing wrongs. One of the Raiders' more controversial reports was the 1971 exposé of state officials in California who were involved in land speculation.

Probably the most important single factor in the shift of emphasis from the preservation of the privileges of the creators of wealth to the protection of the rights of the general public has been the changed attitude of both legislatures and the courts toward personal in-jury. The modern attitude is that *nobody* should be immune to responsibility for injury inflicted on another. Despite the charge by radical groups that the "sys-tem" is so corrupt it is beyond reform and the only solution is to destroy it and start over, the average person in our society has better protection against abuse by the so-called power structure than ever before in history. Even a transient hobo can haul any mammoth corporation into court and force it to pay damages if he can prove that he suffered some kind of compensable damage at its hands.

In order to recover for personal injury, the plaintiff must show that the injury resulted either from a deliberate act or from negligence. In either case it is a tort. A tort is a civil wrong, other than a breach of contract, that constitutes grounds for seeking damages. It does not necessarily have to cause personal injury. Any intentional or negligent act causing a wrong is a tort—for instance, defamation of character or destruction of property—but in this chapter we are concerned only with torts resulting in personal injury.

Just as intent must be shown in criminal law before anyone can be held guilty of a crime, intent is also necessary for an act to be a tort. It is not necessary to show hostile intent, however, to establish that an act was deliberate. A person may have the best of intentions and still be guilty of a tort.

A diabetic suffering from insulin shock was once brought in to the emergency room of a hospital. When the doctor on duty had the man stripped to the waist in order to examine him, he noted a large, open sore, ringed by dead flesh, on the patient's shoulder. (The sores and wounds of diabetics frequently heal very poorly.) Reasoning that if he brought the patient out of shock first, he would have to administer an anesthetic before cutting away the dead flesh, whereas the state the man was in was as effective as an anesthetic, the doctor trimmed the sore with surgical scissors and dressed it before bringing the patient out of shock. Later, when the wound became reinfected and resulted in the patient's hospitalization, he charged the doctor with a tort and brought suit against him for personal injury.

The patient won his suit. The court held that the cutting away of the dead flesh constituted a surgical operation, and even though the doctor's intention had been only to help the patient, he should have revived him first and asked permission to operate. If the injury had been such that delay would have endangered the patient's life, that would have been a different matter, as it could be assumed that such an injury was at least part of the reason the patient had been brought to the hospital; but the patient had entered the hospital for treatment of a specific condition, and the doctor had no right to gratuitously perform an unasked-for operation having no bearing on that condition.

In many cases the motive behind a tort is far from benign, of course. It is even possible for a tort to be also a crime. If you punch your neighbor in the nose, he may have you arrested for the crime of battery, but you have also committed a tort and may be sued in civil court for personal injury.

Wrongs that are unintentional are called *negligent wrongs*. Most damage suits for personal injury charge negligence rather than intention, particularly when insurance is involved, even if the plaintiff may have reason to believe there was an element of intent on the defendant's part. The reason for this is the legal principle that it is against the public interest to allow anyone to benefit from his own malicious acts. Liability insurance does not usually cover damage inflicted with malicious intent. If such intent is established, the insurance company is off the hook, and it is up to the defendant to pay whatever damages are awarded out of his own pocket.

This general rule applies primarily in personal-injury cases arising out of automobile accidents, since insurance is most likely to be involved in those. Whereas many people carry homeowner's insurance that covers their liability for injuries suffered on their property, few carry any liability insurance to cover them when away from home except when driving their automobiles. Nearly everyone carries automobile liability insurance, though, and in a number of states it is compulsory.

Although insurance is not supposed to be mentioned in personal-injury suits, the plaintiff is generally aware when there is insurance and frequently knows just how much coverage the defendant has. As the average driver has far more liability coverage than he has in personal assets, the plaintiff is much more likely to collect whatever award is granted if it comes from the insurance company. He is therefore better off to prove negligence instead of intent in most cases, even if he secretly believes the defendant deliberately ran into him.

Of course, if the insurance company can establish malicious intent, it will do so despite the desires of the plaintiff, since that automatically frees it of any responsibility. A California insurance company fought and won a classic case in California involving this principle a few years back. The insured client drove a self-mixing concrete truck. He suspected his wife of having a lover, and one day as he drove by his own house in his truck, he spotted his rival's convertible parked in front with its top down. On impulse he poured it full of wet concrete up to the tops of the doors.

The rival brought suit for damages and received an award. The defendant carried a liability policy that covered him not only in the event of collision with another vehicle but also for any damage resulting from the pouring of concrete. Nevertheless the insurance company refused to pay on the grounds that this clause was intended to cover accidents, such as mistakenly pouring a driveway at the wrong location, and did not cover damage from deliberately malicious acts. The court sided with the insurance company, and the defendant had to pay the award from his own pocket.

There are, of course, situations in which it is necessary to prove intent before you have a case. Any court would be likely to eye with extreme dubiousness the claim that an assailant "negligently" hit you with a blackjack. Regardless of the insurance carried by the defendant, you would have to charge him with a tort in such an instance if you expected any recovery at all.

There are also cases in which the award received may be higher if intent is established. In addition to *compensatory damages, punitive damages* may be asked for if the injury was maliciously inflicted. If granted, this is a separate award on the top of the primary award. As punitive damages cannot be asked for in negligence suits, there may be a distinct monetary advantage to the plaintiff to attempt to establish malicious intent. Juries may award three different types of damages: nominal, compensatory, and punitive.

Nominal damages are sometimes granted in cases where the defendant has been proved to be at fault, but the plaintiff has not established any appreciable financial loss. Perhaps the plaintiff received a black eye in a barroom fight but required no medical attention and lost no work. To assuage his lost dignity, the jury might award him the nominal damage of one dollar and require the defendant to pay court costs. (For some unknown psychological reason the commonest amount of nominal damage granted by juries is six cents. This seems to strike most people as the epitome of a token sum.)

Compensatory damages are granted in cases where the plaintiff has established actual financial loss. This includes medical bills, loss of wages, and in cases of serious injury or death, often a number of intangibles. When the plaintiff has injuries that may incapacitate him for some time, or permanently, usually doctors on both sides testify as to his precise condition and prognosis, almost invariably giving conflicting testimony. It is up to the jury, or the judge if there is no jury, to decide who to believe and figure out just how long the plaintiff will probably be unable to work. Evidence as to his potential earning capacity, had he not been injured, is then usually presented by the plaintiff's lawyer. It might go like this:

PLAINTIFF'S ATTORNEY: Ladies and gentlemen of the jury, my client started with his present company as a truck dispatcher five years ago, at the age of twenty-five, at one hundred dollars a week. He has since received two promotions and is now route manager at ten thousand dollars a year, or roughly double his starting salary. In the five years his doctors estimate he will be unable to work, it may logically be assumed that he would have again doubled his salary to twenty thousand dollars. Therefore a fair average figure of fifteen thousand dollars a year in lost wages can be computed.

It should further be taken into account that

five years away from his job will automatically place him five years behind on the promotion scale. Even if he is given his old job back, which is at best uncertain, it probably would be at his present salary scale, or ten thousand dollars a year less than he could expect if he had not been incapacitated. He will always be that five years behind, with a resultant loss of ten thousand dollars a year income for the rest of his employable life. We therefore ask that when you consider the subject of wage loss only, you figure it on the basis of fifteen thousand dollars a year for the next five years and ten thousand dollars a year thereafter until my client reaches the retirement age of sixty-five.

The defense lawyer will attack this shifty arithmetic and with equally hypothetical figures make the wage loss come out a fraction of the plaintiff's figure. The jury or judge has to decide which to believe and usually comes up with a compromise figure somewhere between the two.

In cases of death there are equally intangible factors for the jury to consider. If the plaintiff is the widow of the victim, the jury probably will be asked to compute his probable total earnings if he had lived to normal retirement age. It will also be asked to put a precise monetary value on the loss of his companionship and in cases in which there are children to grant additional compensation for "loss of parental guidance." If the plaintiff is the widower of the victim, and she had been a working wife, he could similarly ask compensation for the wages she could have been expected to earn if she had lived, for loss of companionship, and loss of parental guidance for his children.

In addition he could ask to be compensated for the loss of her "services and affection," meaning her homemaking and connubial activities.

Athough setting precise monetary values on such intangibles may seem outrageous (Exactly how many dollars is the loss of a loving mother worth to a three-year-old child?), it should be kept in mind that money is the only thing a judge or jury has to deal with in personal-injury cases—and at least it is fairer than the primitive system of composition, where a set payment was fixed for every type of wrong. Juries and judges have to have *some* rational basis on which to decide awards, and until a better one is devised, lawyers who specialize in personal injury will continue to need to be as skilled in arithmetic as in law. It was largely this type of arithmetical argument that accounted for the previously mentioned large difference in two awards granted by different juries in suits involving the same airplane crash. The jury trying the case of the young married couple who died in the crash had to figure the deceased husband's earning capacity by starting with the basic factor that he had been earning fifteen thousand dollars a year when he died. The other jury had to consider the potential lifetime earnings of a man who had been accustomed to swinging million-dollar deals.

Punitive damages constitute a separate award on top of compensatory damages. They are not often asked for in personal-injury cases, because the defendant's insurance is too often a vital factor in such cases. They are most common in suits for defamation of character. In a defamation-of-character suit it is first necessary to prove that the defendant committed slander or libel.

The former is defamation by spoken words or gestures. The latter is publication of defamatory matter in writing or printing or graphic representation of defamatory matter in pictures, cartoons, or even statues. "Publication" in this sense does not mean the matter has necessarily received wide circulation. It is merely the act of communicating defamatory matter to one or more persons. Thus a letter written to your mother criticizing your mother-in-law could be libelous.

After slander or libel has been proved, it is then necessary to prove that the act was harmful to the plaintiff, but proving both these things merely lays the ground for asking for compensatory damages. In order to collect punitive damages in addition, the plaintiff must prove that the defendant deliberately broadcast the defamatory matter with the intention of harming him and was not merely an irresponsible gossip. Similarly, in the rare instances when punitive damages are asked for in personal-injury suits, malicious intent must be shown. Such instances are restricted almost entirely to cases of personal assault or to cases where injury resulted from the setting of booby traps.

One of the problems juries face in personal-injury suits is that once they fix an award, neither the plaintiff nor the defendant has any recourse if the plaintiff's condition thereafter undergoes a marked change. Appellate courts are empowered to reduce awards and often do, but once the case has been reviewed and the final amount is fixed, nothing can change it. A jury grants compensatory damages of $1,000,000 to a plaintiff shown to be permanently paralyzed. The appellate court cuts the award to $500,000, and this final judgment is entered. The next day the plaintiff miraculously recovers full use of all his limbs. The defendant has no legal recourse to get the award further reduced.

It works the other way too, however. Another plaintiff receives a modest award for injuries that are apparently only minor. After the final judgment is entered, his condition steadily deteriorates until he is totally disabled. He cannot again go back into court and sue for an increased amount.

The workmen's compensation laws of the various states have got around this disadvantage insofar as industrial accidents are concerned by providing that compensation cases may be reopened when there is a change in condition. Furthermore, in most states workmen's compensation awards are handled by special administrative agencies, usually called state workmen's compensation boards, separate from the state courts. There is an element of the ancient institution of composition in the workmen's compensation laws, in that they fix specific sums for every type of injury: so much for the loss of a little finger, a different amount for the loss of a ring finger, more for the loss of a thumb than for any other finger. Workmen's compensation is designed to free the courts from litigation arising from industrial accidents and also to protect workers from impoverishment resulting from such accidents. Prior to workmen's compensation it was necessary for a worker to prove negligence by his employer before he could collect for an on-the-job injury, with the result that if he lost his case, he made no recovery even if permanently disabled. Under workmen's compensation in most states awards are granted regardless of whose fault the accident was, with the exception of suicide attempts or, in some states, accidents due to drunkenness.

It is grounds for the defense to ask for dismissal of

a personal-injury suit if the plaintiff accidentally reveals that the real defendant in the case is an insurance company. The thinking behind this is that juries tend not to worry very much about the size of judgments insurance companies have to pay, and the plaintiff therefore has an unfair psychological advantage if the jury realizes that whatever award it gives is not going to cost the defendant of record anything. Usually the jury is quite aware that the defendant is insured, even though that fact goes unmentioned. It would take a very naïve juror not to suspect that a major airline being sued for a plane crash didn't carry some kind of liability insurance, and he wouldn't have to be very astute to figure out that a common laborer being sued for $100,000 for injuries to a pedestrian he ran over in his automobile probably carried liability insurance in that amount.

The myth has to be maintained that the defendant of record is going to be required to pay any award out of his own pocket, though—unless the *defense* makes the slip that an insurance company is involved. As the plaintiff cannot be penalized for mistakes made by the defense, such a slip is no grounds for dismissal, and the information remains in the record. Sometimes the plaintiff's lawyer will deliberately maneuver a defense witness into revealing that an insurance company is handling the defense. This is considered fair tactics.

Years ago I sat on a six-man municipal court jury in upstate New York hearing an automobile damage suit. The plaintiff was seeking $350 in damages from a woman who had backed out of a blind driveway into the side of his car. There had been no personal injury, the requested damages being for property damage only.

The defendant was not contesting fault but only the

amount of damages, claiming that $290 was adequate. The claim was based on the state law requiring the responsible party in an automobile accident to restore the injured party's car only to its previous condition or if it is not restorable, to pay an amount equal to the car's "Blue Book" retail value prior to the accident. (The "Blue Book" is an official guide for used-car dealers published annually which lists the average wholesale and retail value of used cars.) The defense in this case argued that it was an old car, and therefore new replacement parts were not required under the law. The plaintiff's figure of $350 was based on the cost of brand-new parts. The defense figure of $290 was based on the cost of used parts.

The defense put on the stand as an expert witness a man who testified that he had worked for a series of automobile-repair garages and a couple of automotive-supply stores over a period of years and was therefore familiar with the costs of both new and used parts. The witness then read off a list of the parts necessary for this particular repair job, gave the retail prices of new parts, and then compared them with the prices of used parts he had located in various junk yards. The prices of the used parts came to $60 less than the total for new parts.

The attorney for the plaintiff cross-examined. For convenience we will designate him as "plaintiff," the opposing lawyer as "defense," and the man on the stand, whom we will give the fictional name of Mr. Jones, as "witness." The cross-examination went like this:

PLAINTIFF: Are you a personal friend of the defendant, Mr. Jones?
WITNESS: No, sir.

PLAINTIFF: Are you even acquainted with her?
WITNESS: Oh, yes.
PLAINTIFF: How long have you known her?
WITNESS: Just a few weeks.
PLAINTIFF: Had you ever met her prior to the accident?
WITNESS: No, sir.

At this point the defense attorney objected on the grounds that the relationship between the defendant and the witness had no bearing on the latter's qualifications as an expert. The plaintiff's attorney explained to the court, and to the jury, that his line of questioning was induced by curiosity as to why the witness had gone to all the trouble of running around to junk yards to price used parts for a woman he barely knew. The court admonished counsel that the subject didn't seem pertinent, and that he should drop it. The questioning resumed on another note:

PLAINTIFF: You have testified to working for several employers in either the repair business or the automotive-supply business during recent years, Mr. Jones, but I noted that your employment résumé stopped short about a year and a half ago. Are you still working in one of these fields?
WITNESS: No, sir.
PLAINTIFF: Do you mind telling us your present employment?
DEFENSE: Object as immaterial and irrelevant. The witness's background over a period of years clearly establishes him as an expert in his field. It doesn't matter what he does now.
PLAINTIFF: Your honor, I think it does. Even an expert can become rusty if he doesn't use his

specialized knowledge over a period of time, and I think the jury should know if the witness has for the past year and a half been in some field totally unrelated to his alleged expertise. For all we know he has been working as a ballet dancer during that period and has forgotten everything he knew about automotive parts.

JUDGE: The question seems reasonable. You will have to answer it, Mr. Jones.

PLAINTIFF: I will repeat the question. What is your present employment, Mr. Jones?

WITNESS: [reluctantly] I'm an investigator.

PLAINTIFF: What do you investigate?

WITNESS: [after a lengthy pause, during which he glanced at the defense attorney but got no help] Insurance claims.

The jury in this case was so irritated at the insurance company for taking up the time of six jurors, two lawyers, various witnesses, and the court personnel in an attempt to save $60 that we sent a message to the judge asking if it was possible to award the plaintiff more than he had asked for. When we were informed that it wasn't, we gave him his $350.

Juries are also not supposed to take into account any insurance carried by the plaintiff. The fact that a widow suing an airline for the death of her husband in a plane crash has already collected $200,000 in flight insurance and $50,000 in life insurance has no bearing on her claim against the airline. Similarly the fact that an injured plaintiff's medical expenses were paid in full by a medical insurance policy he carried does not lessen the responsibility of the defendant to reimburse him for his medical costs. The principle here is that plaintiffs with foresight enough to insure themselves against disaster should not be penalized for their foresight, nor should defendants benefit by it.

Juries are sometimes instructed by the court that damage judgments are tax exempt, but this implication that the plaintiff will get to keep all of whatever award he is granted is not quite accurate. As a matter of courtesy within the legal fraternity it is never mentioned by anyone in court that the plaintiff's lawyer's fee will come out of the award. Nearly all personal-injury cases are on a contingency-fee basis. That is, the lawyer agrees to handle the case for a certain percentage of the award, plus expenses. If he loses the case, he gets nothing.

Depending on the locality and the lawyer, contingency fees vary anywhere from 25 percent to 50 percent. The legal profession is a little reticent about releasing figures on the subject, but probably a majority of contingency fees are 50 percent of the award, which means the lawyers get as much out of the suits as the plaintiffs—slightly more, as a matter of fact, since expenses come out of the plaintiff's slice. The legal profession defends this practice on two grounds.

First, spokesmen point out that most plaintiffs in personal-injury suits could not afford to bring suit if they had to hire lawyers strictly on a fee basis. Since all the financial risk is taken by the lawyers, they regard such suits essentially as business partnerships in which the plaintiff supplies the marketable idea and the lawyer furnishes the know-how and the financial backing. Most lawyers who specialize in personal injury sincerely feel that their contribution is worth 50 percent. Second, the legal profession stresses that contingency fees are collected only when the case is won, and when a lawyer loses a case, he not only collects no fee but must also pay the trial expenses himself.

Many specialists in the field insist that even when 50 percent contingency fees are charged, what lawyers actually collect on the average when lost fees and the expenses of unsuccessful cases are deducted is closer to 25 percent.

Because it is difficult to get precise figures from the legal profession, no one really knows what the average split is between plaintiffs and lawyers in personal-injury suits. The only comprehensive survey made in recent years was by the Federal Judicial Center for the year 1968, and its study was limited to personal injuries arising out of automobile accidents. It found that the victims of 220,000 automobile-accident injuries who received awards that year were granted $1,400,000,000. Plaintiffs collected a total of $700,000,000. Legal fees, over and above expenses, amounted to $600,000,000. (The other $100,000,000 went for expenses.) This figure included fees for both plaintiffs' and defense lawyers, however, with no breakdown between them. It may be assumed that the lion's share went to plaintiffs' lawyers, though, since most defenses in personal-injury suits are handled by lawyers who work for insurance companies on retainer fees, and their incomes from handling such suits hardly approach what the plaintiffs' lawyers earn when they win them. Even if you arbitrarily assume that $500,000,000 of the $600,000,000 in legal fees went to plaintiffs' attorneys, the average contingency fee works out to only a little over 40 percent instead of 50 percent.

Recently there has been widespread discussion of "no-fault" insurance for automobile accidents. Under this system your own insurance would compensate you for personal injuries suffered in an accident, regardless of fault. The theory is that in the long run insurance costs would be no greater, and the courts would be freed of the main cause of their congestion.

So far, although a number of state legislatures have considered no-fault insurance laws, only five have so far passed such laws, and in one of those—Illinois—the state supreme court has declared the law unconstitutional. In none of the other four does the no-fault plan give complete coverage. In Massachusetts, whose 1970 law was the first in the country, the act provides for automatic settlement of claims up to $2,000. Larger claims must still be settled by litigation. Proponents of the Massachusetts plan hail it as a success; opponents call it a disaster. The former point to a substantial reduction in insurance-premium costs within the state as evidence of its success; the latter counter that premiums are down only because awards are down, which they claim is the result of plaintiffs not collecting the amount of damages they should under the plan.

The plans in Delaware and Oregon are even more limited than the Massachusetts plan. Florida's, which went into effect January 1, 1972, is the most comprehensive to date. It provides for compulsory no-fault coverage and prohibits actions except for serious injury or economic loss of more than $5,000. Suits for "pain and suffering" may still be filed in cases of serious injury or death or if medical bills run over $1,000. Damage to automobiles up to $550 is paid without legal action. Similar legislation is under consideration in several other states, including New York and California, and at this writing bills have been introduced into both the United States Senate and the House of Representatives to provide for a nationwide plan of no-fault insurance.

Chapter 7

COURT PROCEDURES

The first thing a lawyer has to do when a client engages him to start a legal action is to figure out the deadline for bringing suit. Every state has enacted *statutes of limitations* for certain crimes and for *all* civil actions. That is, the law requires that persons accused of crimes, other than a few felonies such as murder, where there is no statute of limitations, must be charged within a specified period of time, or they may thereafter not be brought to trial at all. Similarly a civil suit must be brought within a specified time after the defendant committed the act for which the plaintiff is asking relief. If the deadline passes before the suit is filed, there is no cause for action.

Statutes of limitations vary greatly from state to state and vary just as much within states for different types of actions. The shortest limitations are for claims against governmental entities, which in some states are only ninety days. The shortest limitations in the country for actions against individuals are those for slander in North Carolina and Tennessee. In both states suit must be brought within six months of the alleged slander. Most other states allow either one or two years to bring slander suits, and two—Delaware and New Mexico—allow three years. Statutes of limitations on personal-injury suits range from one to six years in different states. Deadlines for bringing other types of actions vary all the way from one year to twenty.

Nine out of ten personal-injury suits are settled out of court. A large number of other types of damage suits are settled by negotiations between opposing lawyers without ever going to trial too. Some lawyers make a practice of filing suit before starting pretrial negotiations even when they think there is a good chance for settlement out of court, on the theory that this puts them in a better bargaining position by letting the opposition know they mean business. Others prefer to save their clients the expense of drawing up and filing the necessary documents until it seems likely suit is going to have to be brought.

In the latter instance it behooves the lawyer to mark the statutory deadline for filing on his calendar. In 1970 an Oxnard, California, law firm found itself confronted with a major lawsuit by a former client because they were still negotiating for an out-of-court settlement with an insurance company in a personal-injury suit when the one-year deadline for bringing suit passed. The former client sued for what he claimed he could have gotten from the insurance company if his lawyers had kept track of the date.

The second thing a lawyer has to do is decide which court has jurisdiction. Filing suit in the wrong court is grounds for the defense to ask for dismissal and may be a bar to then bringing suit in the proper court. There is also the question of which court to file in when there is more than one of the same type in different localities—for instance, in a case where the jurisdiction clearly lies in a federal district court, but the plaintiff resides in California and the defendant in Missouri, or where the New York State supreme court clearly has jurisdiction, but the plaintiff lives in Buffalo and the defendant in New York City, at opposite ends of the state.

In general the rule on both the federal and state level is that response should be made convenient to the defendant. Thus when the litigants in a case where a federal district court has jurisdiction are both residents of the same state but live in different court districts, the suit must be brought in the district where the defendant resides. In most cases in the state courts suit must be brought in the defendant's county of residence (except when real property is at issue, and then the courts in the county where the property is located generally have jurisdiction, even if neither litigant is a resident).

When the defendant is a corporation, federal law permits suit to be brought in the federal district in which it is incorporated or in any federal district in which it does business. Since for many corporations—such as auto manufacturers and common carriers—this includes every square inch of the fifty states, the law originally resulted in a certain amount of nuisance tactics by plaintiffs. Such devices were used as bringing suit in the United States district court of Alaska for a rail accident in California, with the deliberate intent of making it difficult for the railroad to provide defense witnesses.

In 1948 Congress ended this practice by enacting a law empowering the judges of district courts where such suits were brought to transfer them to any other district court eligible for jurisdiction, if such transfer was deemed to be more convenient for the litigants and witnesses. It most states corporations may be held to answer only in counties where they maintain offices or business establishments. In a few, though, apparently on the assumption that the convenience of a state's citizens is more important than that of impersonal corporations, suit may be filed in any county the plaintiff pleases.

In diversity-of-citizenship cases the rules become a little more complicated. When the litigants reside in different states, the plaintiff has the choice, both in the federal courts and on the state level, of bringing suit where either he or the defendant lives. If he chooses to suit his own convenience by filing in his own state, however, he has the problem of serving process on a nonresident.

Service of process is the third thing lawyers have to think about in filing suits on behalf of clients.

SERVICE OF PROCESS

Just as it is a fundamental principle of criminal law that an accused person must be informed of the charges against him before he can be brought to trial, it is a fundamental principle of civil law that a defendant must be notified of any action against him before a plaintiff has the right to ask for legal remedy. Such notification is known as *service of process*. In most states for most types of cases, this notification must be personally delivered to the defendant in writing and is called a *summons*. The summons states the type of action filed by the plaintiff, the name and location of the court where it is being filed, and decrees that answer to the plaintiff's claim must be made within a specified time, or the defendant will lose the case by default.

Usually such summonses are delivered by special officers of the court, most often called marshals, but in some states sheriff's deputies or other police officers perform this function. When publicly paid officers are used, the fees for process-serving are added to the court costs. A few states allow professional process-servers who perform this service for fees. In these states the plaintiff's lawyer hires such a process-server and adds the cost to his legal fee.

Personal service is not required in all cases. In the federal courts delivery of written notice to the defendant's domicile is sufficient, providing the domicile is within the jurisdiction of the court. In a number of states delivery to anyone who answers the door at the defendant's domicile is allowable. In a couple of states it is even legal to mail summonses.

The disadvantage for the plaintiff in a diversity-of-citizenship case who chooses to make it convenient for himself at the expense of the defendant's convenience by filing suit where he resides instead of where the defendant lives is that process has to be served within the geographic limits of the court's jurisdiction. This means that the process-server in a federal case must catch the defendant within the plaintiff's judicial district. This may be no appreciable problem if the defendant does business there or frequently visits the area, but if he has no particular reason to travel to that judicial district, it may be impossible to serve papers on him. This situation often forces a plaintiff to change his mind and file the suit in the defendant's judicial district, where there will be no service problem.

Similarly, in suits brought in the state courts, process in most cases must be served within the boundaries

of the state where the suit has been filed. There are
some exceptions to this, however. If the defendant is
a resident of the state and has deliberately left the
court's jurisdiction to avoid service of process, he may
be served anywhere the process-server is able to locate him. Another exception is in automobile-accident
cases. Special legislation in all fifty states gives the
courts of the state where an accident takes place jurisdiction in civil disputes arising out of such an accident.
This legislation includes the right of the state attorney
generals to have process served on defendants no matter where they reside. Under most state laws it is sufficient notice merely to mail such summonses. In most
diversity-of-citizenship cases, however, process must
be served within the geographic limits of the court's
jurisdiction, which frequently forces the plaintiff to
bring suit in enemy country, despite his supposed
choice of bringing it either where he or the defendant
resides.

In some types of cases, notably in divorce actions,
service by publication is deemed to be adequate notice
to the defendant. A notice announcing the plaintiff's
action, containing the same information as in a summons, is placed in the classified section of a newspaper
of general circulation within the jurisdiction of the
court. This device is used primarily when the defendant's whereabouts are unknown.

This is the customary procedure in Nevada divorces
in cases of desertion. A typical case would be that of
a woman who moves from New York City to Reno for
six weeks in order to meet the residence requirement
for divorce. Her husband walked out on her six months
previously, and she has no idea where he is. The lawyer she engages arranges for publication of the usual

notice in a Reno newspaper. The odds of her husband ever seeing this notice are about the same as making a living by playing Reno slot machines. This is presumed, though, to constitute "all reasonable effort" to inform the defendant of the action against him.

When the defendant is a corporation instead of an individual, the same general rules for serving process apply, and service is made upon some officer of the corporation.

PRELIMINARY PROCEDURES

Once a plaintiff has definitely decided to file suit, there are certain procedures his lawyer must follow. His first move is to file with the clerk of the court that will have jurisdiction in the case a document that is variously called a *complaint*, a *petition*, or a *statement*, depending on where the attorney is practicing law. For purposes of simplicity we will hereafter refer to this document as the complaint. On the outside cover of the complaint is typed the name of the court in which the suit is being filed and the title of the action. Every lawsuit has a specific title by which it is forever afterward known in the event that lawyers wish to cite it as a precedent in future trials.

On page 153 is the way the cover of a complaint might read in the case of a man asking damages for injuries sustained when a subway door closed on him. In such cases it is customary to name as defendants both the corporation that is the common carrier and the employee whose alleged negligence was responsible for the injury. The Ralph Smith mentioned is the subway guard the plaintiff claims prematurely caused the doors to close.

The body of the complaint contains a statement of

Civil Court of the City of New York

....

Richard Jones,

                                    Plaintiff

                    Vs.

Municipal Transit Authority of New
York City, a corporation, and Ralph
Smith,

                            Defendants

---

the plaintiff's claim, specifies the remedy requested, naming an amount if the remedy asked is a monetary judgment, and usually includes the residence of all parties concerned. In some jurisdictions the complaint also summarizes the facts of the case, but in courts where the Federal Rules of Practice are followed, this is unnecessary. The feeling is that the facts can be developed during the trial, and all the complaint need state is the claim.

In many cases, particularly where the action is merely a request for a money judgment against a debtor, this is the only document filed by either side. If the defendant makes no reply, the court will simply enter a judgment by default, and the case is over. If the defendant decides to contest the claim, however, he will have his attorney file a *plea* or *answer,* but first the attorney may think it worthwhile to file a *demurrer.*

A demurrer is a motion for dismissal on the grounds

that the plaintiff does not have proper grounds to bring suit. In effect what it says is that even if everything the plaintiff claims proves to be true, he has no case. The reasons for demurring can vary from the claim that the suit has been filed in the wrong jurisdiction to the claim that the contract on which the suit is based is fraudulent. Here is an example:

An importer of leather goods brings suit against a New York City department store for breach of contract. The department store ordered a thousand alligator bags, then refused delivery. The defendant demurs that the sale of alligator bags is illegal in New York City and that the plaintiff was aware of this when he induced a representative of the store to sign the order. The court would probably grant the motion in this case, on the grounds that the contract was fraudulent.

A few years back it was almost routine for defendants' lawyers to file demurrers in attempts to get suits dismissed on various technicalities. The practice has diminished considerably, however, largely because the courts look with increasing disfavor on attempts by lawyers to win cases on legal technicalities instead of on merits. Demurrers are still occasionally filed, and cases still get dismissed because of them.

If the motion for dismissal is denied, the defendant may still file an answer. The answer, also in writing, may admit the plaintiff's claim but allege extenuating circumstances. It may deny the claim, and it may include a counterclaim. For instance, when the plaintiff is an interior decorator who is suing to collect for painting the rooms of a house, the defendant's answer may admit that the paint job was performed and was not paid for, but he may submit the counterclaim that the plaintiff ruined an expensive rug by getting paint on it. The plaintiff may file a *reply* to the defendant's answer, giving arguments against whatever allegations were made in the answer counter to the allegation in the complaint.

In many lawsuits there is no dispute concerning the facts but only about the interpretation of the law. That is, both sides agree as to the circumstances but disagree as to the legal responsibilities of the parties concerned. In such cases, at any point of the proceedings so far outlined, the judge may enter a *summary judgment* in favor of one party or the other. In effect, in a summary judgment the court says that there is no point in scheduling a full scale trial, since all the judge is going to be asked to do at the end of the trial is to rule on the questions of law, and the documents so far submitted already give him sufficient information to make such rulings.

A bank sues to collect a $500 note. The debtor files an answer admitting the debt but claiming that the bank employee who approved the loan informed him verbally that it wouldn't matter if he paid it three months late. Instead of waiting for the case to come to trial, the bank applies to the court for a summary judgment on the grounds that the bank employee, since fired, had no authority to make such a statement and that there is a written bank directive forbidding such verbal exceptions to the written terms of notes accepted by the bank. In all probability the court would grant a summary judgment in favor of the bank in this case.

If there are questions of fact which will have to be decided by a judge or a jury, and the opposing sides cannot reach a settlement agreement, trial will be scheduled, but pending trial, the plaintiff may make one more preliminary move if he feels it necessary by applying for a *conservatory remedy*. Conservatory remedies have the purpose of protecting the plaintiff's interests while his suit is pending. A plaintiff asking the court for a judgment declaring that a piano in the possession of his brother-in-law lawfully belongs to him will want to make sure his brother-in-law doesn't sell it before the case comes to trial. He will therefore ask the court for a *temporary restraining order* forbidding the sale of the piano until its ownership is ruled upon. In a simple case such as this, where there seems no reason to believe the order will cause any particular inconvenience to the defendant, an affidavit submitted to the court by the plaintiff is usually sufficient to obtain a temporary restraining order, but in many cases such an order can cause considerable inconvenience.

Assume, for instance, that the plaintiff is the Seven-Up Company, and the defendant is the manufacturer of a new drink called Seven-Upp. The plaintiff files for an injunction to prohibit the defendant from continuing to use the name Seven-Upp on the grounds of unfair competition. It may take months or even years for the case to come to trial, and the Seven-Up Company has no intention of allowing its competitor to continue to use the similar name in the interim. Seven-Up's attorneys therefore also apply for a temporary restraining order to halt the use of the name Seven-Upp immediately.

Even though it may seem quite evident that the new company is deliberately attempting to cash in on the goodwill benefits of Seven-Up, until the matter is adjudicated, the defendant cannot be held guilty of unfair competition. In the event that the eventual decision is that he has every legal right to use the name

Seven-Upp, his interests must be protected pending trial. The court therefore appends to the temporary restraining order the condition that the Seven-Up Company must post sufficient bond to compensate the defendant for the inconvenience of being forced to change his product's name if he eventually wins the right to change the name back to Seven-Upp again. The purpose of requiring bond in such cases is not only to protect the defendant's rights but also to discourage legal harassment. A spiteful plaintiff is likely to think twice before asking for a temporary restraining order whose purpose is merely to cause the defendant inconvenience if the plaintiff realizes an eventual adverse ruling is likely to cost him money.

The Federal Rules of Civil Procedure, which are part of the Federal Rules of Practice and were drawn up by the Supreme Court and approved by Congress in 1938, provides for *discovery proceedings* in the federal courts. Most states have adopted similar rules, although in some places they are called *disclosure proceedings*. Under this rule either party to a lawsuit may demand that his opponent produce, before the trial, whatever documents he plans to present in evidence, including, in some states, affidavits taken from witnesses. Legal authorities rather sharply disagree on the wisdom of this practice. Its opponents feel that too often lawyers use the privilege to make "fishing expeditions" in the hope of discovering some weak point on the other side that they can blow up out of all proportion to its importance.

It can also backfire. A few years ago, in a multi-million-dollar suit for damages against the Richardson-Merrell Company for injuries suffered by users of a drug called MER/29 marketed by that company, the motion for discovery by the plaintiffs' lawyer produced more evidence than he cared to wade through. The drug company sent him microfilms of 120,000 separate documents.

Probably more legal authorities favor discovery proceedings than oppose them. The majority feeling is that the disclosure of all the facts before the trial tends to result in suits decided on their merits instead of won or lost by courtroom skill. The practice has considerably lessened the amount of courtroom drama, though. The favorite Hollywood courtroom scene in which one lawyer totally flabbergasts his opponent by suddenly springing a bit of unexpected evidence is almost a thing of the past in real life. It is very hard to surprise an opponent who has been permitted to examine all your evidence in advance.

Somewhat similar to discovery proceedings is the request for a *bill of particulars,* but instead of asking for the disclosure of evidence, this merely asks for more specific details about the claim. For example, in the previously mentioned auto damage case on which I sat as a juror and in which the plaintiff was asking for $350, the defense asked for a bill of particulars before the trial. This required the plaintiff to submit an affidavit listing the make, model, year, and mileage of the damaged automobile, a list of the parts requiring replacement, and the estimated labor cost for repair. It was on the basis of this bill of particulars that the defense contested the amount claimed and tried to settle for $60 less.

PRETRIAL CONFERENCE

Since the beginning of the legal profession it has been customary for lawyers to get together with opposing lawyers before trial in attempt to reach out-of-court settlements. The practice of judges calling such conferences and presiding over them is a relatively new development in legal history, though. As nearly as I can determine, the first place in this country where the pretrial conference was used on a regular basis was in Detroit. In 1929 the judges of that city began regularly calling conferences in their chambers with attorneys for both sides in cases where the judges felt there were reasonable chances of reaching settlements. In these conferences the judge stepped down from his usual role of trial referee to act as an impartial adviser to the lawyers and the litigants for the purpose of helping them reach settlements or if this proved impossible, at least of working out ways to simplify the trial.

The Detroit experiment had such a dramatic effect on court congestion that it caused nationwide attention. Numerous state bar associations sent representatives to the city to study the system. Nevertheless the procedure spread rather slowly until after 1938, when Congress approved the New Federal Rules of Civil Procedure. Rule 16 provides:

> In any action, the court may in its discretion direct the attorneys for the parties to appear before it in conference to consider: (1) the simplification of the issues, (2) the necessity or desirability of amendments to the pleadings, (3) the possibility of obtaining admissions of fact and of documents which will avoid unnecessary proof, (4) the limitation of the number of expert witnesses, (5) the advisability of a preliminary reference of issues to a master for findings to be used as evidence when the trial is to be by jury,

(6) such other matters as may aid in the disposition of the action.

Thereafter the use of the pretrial conference in state courts spread more quickly and is now routine in the majority of states.

There are, of course, many cases where it is apparent there can be no basis for a negotiated settlement. The plaintiff suing his brother-in-law for possession of a piano, for instance, is hardly likely to be willing to accept just the piano stool as a compromise settlement. No judge would waste his time or that of the litigants by scheduling a pretrial conference in such a case for the sole reason of attempting to reach a settlement, although he might hold one to attempt to simplify the trial. In damage suits, however, particularly when some intangible factor such as loss of reputation is a factor, there is almost always room to negotiate. The modern tendency is for judges to call pretrial conferences in nearly all such cases when the opposing lawyers have been unable to reach settlement on their own.

IN THE COURTROOM AT LAST

Eventually the one out of ten civil cases which does not end in dismissal, summary judgment, or out-of-court settlement reaches the stage of courtroom trial. Trial procedures in civil suits are identical to those in criminal trials insofar as rules of evidence are concerned. There are some differences in other areas, though.

The plaintiff's lawyer in a civil suit is in somewhat the same position as the prosecutor in a criminal trial. He makes his opening statement first and sums up last. The major difference between criminal and civil trials is that in a criminal trial the prosecutor must convince the jury of the defendant's guilt "beyond reasonable doubt." In a civil suit the jury is required to consider only the *preponderance of evidence.* In other words, the plaintiff does not have to prove beyond question that the defendant wronged him; he merely has to convince the jury that it is more likely than doubtful that he did. Conversely, it is not enough for the defendant to show that he *might* not be at fault; he must convince the jury that he is less likely to be at fault than he is likely to be.

As in criminal cases, juries decide the facts and judges rule on the law. The only exception to this is in Louisiana, where civil juries (but not criminal juries) interpret both facts and law. On appeal, however, the Louisiana court of appeals or the Supreme Court can reverse the rulings of juries in both areas. In actual practice Louisiana lawyers tend to avoid civil juries and prefer to try civil cases before judges only.

In all states and in the federal courts a unanimous verdict is necessary to convict in a criminal case. A number of states have modified this requirement for civil suits. Some require agreement by ten jurors out of twelve, others require nine out of twelve, and one state allows a two-thirds majority to prevail. In the federal courts the jury verdict must be unanimous in all cases involving twenty dollars or more unless the litigants have agreed in advance to accept a verdict by a stipulated majority. A few states that otherwise require unanimous verdicts have adopted similar rules.

When there is no jury and trial is before a judge only, the court must rule on both fact and law. The decision in such cases is rendered in two parts, called *findings of fact* and *conclusions of law.* The former gives the court's decision as to what the circumstances of the dispute are; the latter interprets the law as it applies to those circumstances, including a statement as to the exact form of relief to which the winning litigant is entitled. The judgment is appended to this decision. As a general rule actions in equity are more likely to be tried before judges only; actions in law are more likely to be tried before juries.

In a criminal trial a *directed verdict* of not guilty (but not one of guilty) can be ordered by the judge. In a civil suit the judge may order a directed verdict for either side in any case where he deems the evidence so predominantly in favor of that side that there is really no issue of fact for the jury to vote upon. Such directed verdicts are extremely uncommon for a couple of reasons, though.

First, when the evidence is so lopsidedly in favor of one side, the judge is more likely either to dismiss the case or to render a summary judgment before the case comes to trial. Second, if an appellate court overturns his directed verdict, a whole new trial will be necessary. For the second reason judges are more likely to let juries go ahead and render their verdicts, even when the right seems to be all on one side. Then, if the jury returns a verdict that seems to the judge completely against the evidence, he may order it *set aside*. If an appellate court finds the judge in error, it can merely reinstate the jury's verdict and no new trial will be necessary.

Verdicts handed down by juries in civil cases are of two types: *general verdicts* and *special verdicts*. A general verdict makes an overall decision on all issues. "We find a verdict in favor of the plaintiff for twelve thousand dollars" in a general verdict. "We find no cause of action" or "We find in favor of the defendant" are typical general verdicts for the other side. A special verdict is one in which the jury makes a decision on some specific question whose answer is necessary before the judge can rule on a matter of law. The jury decides on that fact only, then lets the court decide what relief is to be granted.

Some years ago the Westgate Drug Mart, of New York City, advertised for a delivery boy. Late on a Monday afternoon a sixteen-year-old boy applied for the job. He was hired and was told to report for work the next morning. The druggist noted from the address on the boy's application that on the way home he had to pass right by the home of a customer who had ordered a prescription, so the druggist asked the boy to deliver the prescription. En route the boy, riding a bicycle, was struck by a car.

Subsequently the boy's parents applied in his name for a workmen's compensation award on the grounds that he was injured in the course of his employment. The state workmen's compensation board turned him down, ruling that his employment had not yet started at the time of the accident. The boy's parents then took the matter to court.

The jury in this case was asked to render a special verdict solely on the question of whether or not the plaintiff was a bona fide employee of the drugstore when the accident occurred. The verdict was: "We find the plaintiff was an employee of the Westgate Drug Mart at the time of the accident." Nothing more. The matter of fault for the accident or the amount of award, if any, were not the jury's concern. It was required only to answer the specific question asked of it.

It happened that in this case the court's decision, after this question of fact was settled, was strictly limited too. The court ruled merely that the boy was entitled to relief under the workmen's compensation law, but it had no authority to fix an award. That had to be left to the state workmen's compensation board.

Chapter 8

THE CURRENT AND FUTURE
STATUSES OF THE COURTS

In 1906 Roscoe Pound, then dean of the law department of the University of Nebraska and later to become dean of Harvard's law school, shook up the
American Bar Association at its annual convention
with a scathing attack on the "archaic" system of justice in America. Citing congested courts, the waste of
judicial time, unnecessary retrials, and the boredom
of jury duty, he said, "Uncertainty, delay, and expense, and above all the injustice of deciding cases upon points of practice . . . have created a deep-seated
desire to keep out of court, right or wrong, on the part
of every sensible businessman in the community."

During the ensuing two-thirds of a century the
American legal system has made many important
advances. The right of counsel, regardless of ability to
pay, has been firmly confirmed. Procedure has been
modernized. The courts have repeatedly responded to
social issues such as civil rights with just decisions,
often against pressures from powerful forces of reac-
tion. They have strengthened the rights of individuals
against the arbitrary wielding of power by government.
They have given dimension to freedom of speech and
press. They have extended the right of due process—
which has always been available to members of the
"establishment"—to the poor, the black, and even un-

popular exponents of radical philosophies generally rejected by the majority.

The *machinery* of our legal system, far from improving since Roscoe Pound's detailed indictment, has actually deteriorated even more, however. Many of our political and judicial authorities are seriously alarmed that unless widespread reforms are instituted very soon, the entire judicial apparatus may come to a grinding and catastrophic halt, and they warn that we are hurtling toward that disastrous moment at an ever-accelerating rate. These prophets of impending doom are not the sort who ordinarily tend to be alarmist. They include the President of the United States, both the former Chief Justice of the Supreme Court and the present one, and the present Attorney General and most of his living predecessors.

As far back as 1958 Earl Warren, then Chief Justice of the Supreme Court, warned that court delays were "corroding the very foundations of government in the United States." No one paid much attention. Today, in the federal district courts alone, there is a backlog of more than one hundred thousand untried civil and criminal cases. About one-fifth of the criminal cases have been pending more than a year. Civil cases, on the average, take more than thirteen months to come to trial.

Actually this is a rather rosy picture compared to the chaos in the state courts. There the logjam of back cases has become incredible. In the spring of 1971 Chicago's Cook County jail held 1,700 prisoners legally guilty of nothing except inability to raise bail. That was the number awaiting trial, *unconvicted* of anything and therefore, under our system of justice, presumed innocent until they were convicted. More than 100 of the 1,700 had been awaiting trial nearly two years. The officially admitted average wait is six months; prison inmates guess it as closer to a year. In New York City it is not uncommon for prisoners to languish as long as eighteen months in the House of Detention for Men (known as the Tombs) awaiting trial.

In 1970 national census-takers discovered a total of 83,079 persons awaiting trial in city and county jails. This, of course, included only those charged with crimes who were unable to make bail. There are no composite figures available to show the nationwide number of untried criminal cases, but it probably runs ·at least ten times that.

Civil cases everywhere take at least from six months to a year to be heard. More commonly the wait is two years; in some jurisdictions it is up to five years.

The blame for this backlog can be about equally divided between criminal and civil matters. Although this book is concerned with only civil law, the problem is not divisible, because for the most part both types of cases are heard in the same courtrooms by the same judges. Consequently the problem has to be looked at from both angles.

A number of factors in criminal law have contributed to the crisis. One is the spiraling crime rate, which the Federal Bureau of Investigation says has increased 2½ times in the last ten years. Explanations for the increase vary widely, but there is general agreement that the expanding use of drugs has been a contributing factor. Half the criminal cases handled by Los Angeles courts last year were for possession or dealing in drugs. Furthermore the enormous expense of "feeding a habit" drives hard drug users into crimes to get money.

Probably an even greater factor has simply been the

extension of the rights of due process to large groups of the underprivileged who never were previously able to exercise these Constitutionally guaranteed rights because they had no money. Only a dozen years ago long streams of indigent offenders, unrepresented by lawyers, passed through courtrooms and appeared before the bench only long enough to plead guilty and receive sentences; now they are entitled to request public defenders or Legal Aid lawyers. The result has been to greatly increase the court time spent on each case, even when it finally ends in a guilty plea anyway. By obtaining repeated continuances on various grounds, the lawyers giving this free legal service have increased the time necessary to process such cases by three to five times. (The commonest *real* reason for asking for continuances, although never stated, is to obtain time to negotiate with the district attorney for reduced sentences in return for guilty pleas.) This is not meant as a criticism of the defense lawyers' tactics. The previous assembly-line method allowed too short a time and almost totally denied poor defendants their legal rights. The practice is merely cited as one of the contributing factors to the crisis in our courts.

New awareness of their rights has also resulted in a huge increase in the number of convicted criminals demanding appeals. In the past decade the number of appeals heard in the eleven federal courts of appeal alone has jumped from an annual average of four thousand to over ten thousand.

There has been a similar explosion in the number of cases in the area of civil law. One reason for this is the growth of population, which has nearly doubled in the past fifty years. The 1920 census found slightly less than 106,000,000 people living in the United States; the 1970 census found approximately

205,000,000. The increase in the number of civil suits has been greater than might have been expected simply because most of the population growth took place in the urban areas, and overcrowding inevitably results in more people stepping on each other's toes. It is much easier to get into a legal hassle with a neighbor if you share a yard with fifty other tenants than if you are separated from neighbors on either side by fifty feet of lawn.

Added to all this, social and technological changes have both caused an increase in many types of civil cases and have brought forth many new types of cases. Once the stigma attached to divorce kept all but the most desperately unhappy marriages together. (Only recently did I discover that a deceased aunt of mine had been divorced in 1908. All these years my family had carefully concealed the disgrace.) Changed social attitudes have resulted in one out of four marriages ending in the divorce courts. Consumer actions against manufacturers of defective products, medical malpractice suits, and actions against polluters and destroyers of the environment were almost unheard of a generation ago. Today they clog our courts. And of course the ubiquitous automobile has inundated the courts with damage suits.

At a time when the principles of justice have never been higher or stronger, the mechanics are breaking down. Some judges spend whole days in court doing nothing but continuing cases. Others make frantic efforts to reduce the ever-increasing backlogs by running their courts like assembly lines. Around 300 persons a day are arraigned in Manhattan's criminal courts. The record for one day is 416. All across the country there are courts in which cases are continued so often that it is common for witnesses to get tired of appearing and never being called, so they simply stop appearing. Such cases simply collapse and have to be dismissed, with justice for no one.

Suggestions for clearing up the mess in our courtrooms have been numerous. One has been that we should reorder our national priorities and spend more money to create additional courtrooms and hire more judges. Chief Justice Warren Burger has pointed out that the entire cost of the federal judicial system is $128,000,000 a year, whereas the government spends $200,000,000 for a single C-5A military airplane.

Money alone won't solve the problem, however. The whole system cries out for complete overhaul. Although trial procedures have been considerably modernized since Roscoe Pound's day, the mechanics by which courtrooms are run remain very much the same. To quote Chief Justice Burger again: "In the supermarket age we are like a merchant trying to operate a cracker-barrel grocery store with the methods and equipment of 1900."

Consider this incredible item: Until only a couple of years ago the Supreme Court of the United States had no copying machines. The thousands of pages of legal briefs and memos the nine justices had to read each year were typed in ten copies on "flimsies," the last few copies of which were extremely difficult to read. Only since Warren Burger has become Chief Justice has the Court's stenographic section acquired the kind of copying machines that have been routine in the offices of even small businesses for a quarter of a century. The Court now has two, so that our highest justices are no longer required to strain their eyes over seventh, eighth, or ninth carbon copies on tissue paper.

In countless lower courts records are still kept in

longhand in the same type of ledger books that were used in the nineteenth century. These often measure as much as 2 feet by 1½ feet by 4 inches thick and are extremely cumbersome to handle. There are a few scattered courts where the principles of automation are employed, and even a few equipped with computer systems, but they represent only a tiny fraction of our whole judicial system.

One result of this antiquated machinery is that vast amounts of courtroom time are simply wasted. With all the backlog of cases, criminal-court judges in major cities spend up to half their courtroom time merely waiting for people to show up. Overworked prison officials fail to get a prisoner to court until a phone call comes from the court clerk. An arresting officer gets tired after waiting hours for his case to come up, slips out for a cup of coffee, and can't be located when he is called to testify. The defense attorney, who has too many other cases to sit around waiting for one particular case to be called, is in the middle of a defense in city court when his case is called in the general trial court. A witness has become tired of waiting and gone home.

In New York City simple misdemeanor cases are continued four to five times for reasons that could be avoided merely by better planning and organization. The same situation exists in Chicago, Philadelphia, Detroit, and nearly every other major city. Even in Los Angeles, whose courtrooms are relatively better organized than any of the above-mentioned cities, the backlog of cases, both civil and criminal, hovers around forty-five thousand at least partly because of repeated continuances.

Advocates of better advance planning as at least a partial answer to court congestion can point to Chicago's traffic court as an example of the effectiveness of efficient organization. In a city where both the criminal and the civil courts constantly teeter on the brink of total collapse, Chicago's traffic court twice in a row has won the annual American Bar Association award as the most improved big-city system in the nation. Observers from all over the world have come to Chicago to study this system, which processes an average of around five thousand traffic cases a day, makes no one wait, and still gives every defendant a fair hearing.

The secret is a combination of automation and organization. Citations show the exact time cases will be called, and this information is fed into a computer, which regurgitates it to remind the arresting officer to be present at that time too. The computer also produces the defendant's past record of traffic violations, if any, and shows it to the judge on a courtroom TV screen as he gets ready to pass sentence. Since it shows unpaid parking tickets or other unpaid fines too, these are collected on the spot along with whatever the current fine is.

For defendants who can't get to the court at the designated time or who merely wish to get the matter over with, there is an "instant motions" court, open all day, where they can either pay their fines or arrange for other trial dates. For the benefit of defendants who demand jury trials, a jury panel of sixty is kept standing by at all times so that a jury may be seated and a trial conducted on short notice. In contrast it may take up to a year for a traffic offender to get such a jury trial in New York City or Los Angeles.

Judge Raymond Berg, who was assigned as head of Chicago's traffic court four years ago, is largely responsible for this efficient system. In addition to streamlining and automating the traffic court, he talked the city into increasing the number of traffic courtrooms by 2½ times, increasing the prosecuting staff from fourteen to forty, and raising the number of judges from ten to twenty-six. (New York City has eighteen judges to hear three times the number of cases.)

Admittedly it is a much simpler matter to arrange for all those concerned with a case to appear in court at precisely the same time in a traffic case than in a criminal trial or a civil lawsuit. Although most traffic cases require the appearance of only the defendant and the arresting officer, criminal trials and civil suits usually require the simultaneous assemblage of large numbers of people. In a criminal trial the defendant, the prosecutor, and the defense lawyer must be present, plus any witnesses who are to be called. In civil suits both the plaintiff and the defendant are present in most cases, their respective lawyers, and again all the witnesses to be called. Still, although streamlining and automation cannot be expected to eliminate all delay in these more complicated cases, they certainly could be expected to considerably decrease it.

Other suggestions for reducing the general chaos in our courts have come from virtually every prestigious voice in the judiciary and the legal profession from Chief Justice Warren Burger on down. The Chief Justice, mindful that it is not the business of the Supreme Court to tell the lower courts how to run their operations, is always careful to stress that he is not making any recommendations but is merely pointing out alternatives that the lower federal courts and the states might be wise to study. Such is the prestige of his high office, however, that his comments often exert more powerful influence than out-and-out recommendations from others.

As a case in point, on August 10, 1969, in'a speech before the American Bar Association, Justice Burger suggested that it might be worthwhile to consider training court administrators to take over the function of running the purely business end of courtrooms, thus releasing judges from such routine responsibilities as setting trial dates so they could devote all their courtroom time to their prime job of administering justice. As an analogy he pointed out that long ago hospitals turned over the business of running their facilities to professional administrators who were not doctors in order to relieve doctors of all responsibility except practicing medicine, and the system had proved its efficiency. As a direct result of Justice Burger's comments, which were couched in terms that suggested only a study of the possibility of such a program, the American Bar Association, the American Judicature Society, and the Institute of Judicial Administration got together, set up a board of directors headed by former Attorney General Herbert Brownell, and arranged for the first class of a six-month course in courtroom administration to begin at the University of Denver in May of 1970. The first graduates, most of whom were immediately hired by state courts, finished the course on December 12, 1970, only sixteen months after the Chief Justice brought up the matter.

Legal authorities are generally agreed that one method to reduce considerably the overcrowding of our courtrooms would be to remove certain types of cases from them which could as effectively, or more effectively, be handled in other manners. For instance, it would enormously reduce the burden on our criminal courts to remove from them what *Playboy* magazine, in a continuing editorial campaign for fairer laws which has been going on for some years, calls "crimes without victims." One of these is drunkenness, which accounts for one-third of all arrests in the country. There is almost unanimous agreement among both law-enforcement officials and judicial authorities that drunkenness should be approached as a medical problem instead of as a legal one, yet all across the nation parades of drunks continue to file past inferior-court judges, who hand out sentences long enough to "dry them out." Habitual drunkards sometimes accumulate records of hundreds of such convictions.

Some communities *are* trying a medical approach, with varying degrees of success. One worth noting is in Oxnard, California, where drunks picked up by the police are given the choice of being booked for drunkenness or of voluntarily going to a privately run center for the rehabilitation of alcoholics, where they must agree to stay until sober. So far the result has been a drastic reduction of court time previously taken up by drunk cases, plus the rehabilitation of at least some alcoholics.

Other crimes without victims which it has been suggested could be handled in more effective ways outside of the courtroom include prostitution, gambling, and possession or being under the influence of drugs. (Most authorities believe trafficking in drugs should remain a crime.) Suggestions on how to get them out of the courtroom range all the way from legalizing all three to treating them as medical and psychiatric problems. There is general agreement, though, that trying to deal with them in the courtroom has had no appreciable effect on diminishing any of them as social problems.

In the area of civil law there are several types of cases that could be eliminated from the courts also. Judge Samuel Silverman, of New York's surrogate court, says: "Nine hundred and ninety-nine out of a thousand wills are perfectly all right. So why not just file the things, the way you do a deed for the sale or transfer of property? Why do you have to treat a will as though it was a lawsuit?"

Many legal authorities agree with him. Most wills could be handled more quickly than at present, and at considerably less expense, by an administrative probate office that would simply file them and issue the necessary authorizations for the transfer of property to heirs and the release of bank accounts and safe-deposit boxes. Contested wills would still have to go through the courts, of course, but as Judge Silverman pointed out, that would be about one in a thousand.

Divorce is another legal process that could easily be eliminated from the courts. The nine out of ten divorce cases that are uncontested could be handled by administrative arbitration. Again, contested cases and probably also those where the welfare of children is involved would remain in the courts.

The elimination of one type of case would instantly reduce suits for personal injury by 75 percent: personal injury resulting from automobile accidents. A method to accomplish this—the no-fault insurance plan mentioned in Chapter 6—has been available for over forty years. It was that long ago that the plan was first devised at the Columbia University Law School, but so far it has been accepted by only a few states.

In principle the plan is similar to workmen's compensation. The actual out-of-pocket expenses of an accident—repairs, property damage, and medical bills —would be paid victims by their own insurance companies. In addition awards for loss of work and set amounts for permanent injuries would be made in a manner similar to workmen's compensation awards, again by the victims' own insurance companies. Negligence would not be an issue, and court action would be entirely eliminated.

Up until relatively recently the big block to no-fault insurance was that the legal profession opposed it. This was hardly surprising, since large numbers of lawyers depended on automobile personal-injury cases for the major parts of their incomes. Senator Robert Taft, Jr., of Ohio, speaking to the Cincinnati Bar Association in April of 1971, said, "Unquestionably this reform might have an adverse impact upon the income of many attorneys. I do not believe, however, that the legal profession would put itself in the position of placing its possible short-run economic self-interest ahead of the interests of the general public."

At the time it seemed that the Senator's faith in his fellow lawyers' altruism was a bit starry-eyed. (Senator Taft is also a lawyer.) Bar associations and legal societies had been in the forefront of opposition to the measure wherever it had been proposed. It seemed that it was simply not within human nature, even for a professional class with the high ethical standards that the legal profession claimed it maintained, to give up willingly a major source of income for the public good, but in November of 1971 the California State Bar endorsed the general concept of no-fault auto insurance and appointed a committee to draft a plan to be submitted to the state legislature in 1972. It instructed the commitee that the plan drafted must be practical, workable from a casualty-underwriting aspect, and in the public interest.

Previously during the year the California legislature had defeated a no-fault insurance bill, but with the state bar behind the concept, eventual passage of some kind of no-fault insurance plan seems assured. It seems quite likely that other state bar associations will review their thinking on the subject because of the California stand. It may be too much to expect all of them to endorse no-fault insurance, but at the very least, active opposition will probably be dropped by many of them.

Whether this and other needed reforms will be instituted in time to avoid total collapse of our legal system is by no means a certainty, but I personally am optimistic. The first big step in solving any social problem is widespread recognition that the problem exists. It is increasingly evident that not only the authorities responsible for the administration of justice but also the general public have become deeply concerned over the situation. In the United States, lawmakers respond to acute public concern about issues if they want to stay in office, and there is no reason to believe that legislatures in this instance will be any slower in passing the necessary reform bills and making available the necessary funds to institute reforms than they have been in the past when the public became aroused about social issues.

Some of the finest minds in the judiciary and the legal profession are bent to the task of reforming our courts, and the problem is receiving attention from all three branches of government on all levels. It is my own conviction that within a very few years the just-beginning revolution in courtroom operation will be over and the United States will have a smoothly running, streamlined, and automated system in which both criminal and civil justice will be far swifter than it is today.

GLOSSARY

Absolute Divorce: A term used in some states to distinguish termination of a marriage from limited divorce, or mere separation. See also *decree of legal separation* and *divorce.*

Action for an Accounting: A court action to settle the terms of the dissolution of a business or to require accounting from persons entrusted with funds or property belonging to others. Also called a *proceeding for an accounting.*

Acts of Bankruptcy: Any of six specific acts defined by the National Bankruptcy Act as constituting grounds for filing a petition of bankruptcy against a debtor if he has committed one of them.

Adjective Law: Law prescribing remedies and procedures for enforcing legal rights.

Administrator or Administratrix: A person designated by a court to administer an estate when the decedent has died intestate or when the will fails to name an executor.

Admiralty: The branch of law regulating maritime matters.

Adoption: The legal assumption of parental responsibility for a child other than one's own.

Adversary System: The legal system in England, the

United States, and other common-law countries, in which opposing lawyers are pitted against each other in a contest in which, in civil suits, each is ethically obliged to disclose only that evidence favorable to his own client and in which, in criminal trials, the defense lawyer is similarly bound to protect the interests of his client.

Advocate: The lawyer on either side in a trial.

Affidavit: A written statement sworn to before an officer having the authority to administer oaths.

Alimony: A court-decreed support payment by one ex-spouse to the other after divorce or separation.

Annulment: A decree declaring a marriage invalid.

Answer: A defendant's first reply to the complaint filed by the plaintiff. See also *complaint.*

Assumption of Risk: The outmoded legal principle that an employer is relieved of responsibility for injuries when an employee knowingly accepts a hazardous job.

Attachment: A court order to seize the goods or property of a debtor in order to enforce the payment of a debt.

Bench Warrant: A warrant issued by a court in session for the arrest of a person, most often for failure to appear in court.

Bill of Particulars: Specific details about a claim—such as medical bills, amount of property damage, or other basis on which injury is claimed—demanded of a plaintiff by the defendant.

Bill of Sale: A written instrument transferring ownership of personal property.

Bylaws: Rules adopted by an organization or a corporation for its internal government.

Calendar: The schedule of cases to be tried during a term of court.

Case Law: Law based on precedents rather than on legislation.

Cause of Action: The legal basis on which one person brings a lawsuit against another.

Chancery Court: See *court of equity.*

Chattel: Any item of personal property.

Chattel Mortgage: A lien against personal property. Also called a *security agreement.*

Child Support: Payment made by a divorced or separated parent to the party having custody of his or her children for their support, as distinct from alimony, which is for the support of a divorced spouse only.

Clerk of Court: The officer who keeps the records of a court. Also called a *court reporter.*

Comity: The recognition of the laws of one state by another state.

Committee: A person to whom a minor or an incompetent person is committed. Also called a *guardian.*

Common Carrier: An individual or a corporation that transports persons or property for hire.

Common Law: (1) Custom or usage so widespread that it is recognized as having the force of law. (2) Law in general force throughout an entire nation or a specific portion of a nation, such as one of the United States.

Comparative Negligence: The doctrine that a defendant's liability for an injury to the plaintiff may be reduced an amount proportionate to the plaintiff's contributory fault.

Compensatory Damages: The monetary award granted to a plaintiff for injury by the defendant. See also *punitive damages.*

Complaint: The initial document filed by a plaintiff, outlining his claim against the defendant. Also called a *petition* or a *statement.*

Composition: A primitive system of compensation for damages which decrees a fixed compensation for each type of wrong to be paid the wronged party by the wrongdoer.

Conclusions of Law: The judge's interpretation of the law as it applies to the circumstances of a case, including a statement of the form of relief the winning litigant is entitled to. See also *findings of fact*.

Concurrent Jurisdiction: A situation in which two courts, such as a federal district court and a state trial court, each have jurisdiction in a matter, and a plaintiff has the choice of filing suit in either.

Contempt of Court: An act in defiance of a court order, one that disrupts proceedings, or one that obstructs justice.

Contingency Fee: A legal fee computed on the basis of a percentage of the amount of damages awarded a plaintiff, the understanding being that if there is no award, no fee will be charged.

Contract: A mutual agreement between two or more parties which binds them to a performance and in which each acquires a right to what the other or others promise.

Contributory Negligence: The doctrine that if a plaintiff is even slightly responsible for an injury, no recovery may be made, even if the major fault is the defendant's.

Copyright: The exclusive right of publication or reproduction granted an author or an artist by the federal government for his artistic production for a certain number of years.

Counterclaim: A claim presented by a defendant which is designed to refute or diminish the plaintiff's claim.

Court of Equity: A supplemental court whose purpose is to administer justice on the basis of reasonableness when the law fails to supply a solution to a legal problem. Also called a *chancery court*. See also *equity*.

Court Reporter: See *clerk of court*.

Creditor: One to whom a debt is owed.

Damages: Compensation paid to a plaintiff by the defendant for injury to plaintiff's person, property, or rights.

Declaratory Judgment: A decree defining the rights of the parties in a contract or an agreement when there is no claim for damages or other relief.

Decree: A written judgment or determination by a court.

Decree of Legal Separation: A decree, usually issued at the request of only one party to a marriage, permitting the spouses to live apart and limiting their responsibility to each other. Also called a *judicial separation*, a *limited divorce*, or *separate maintenance*. See also *absolute divorce*.

Decree of Specific Performance of Contract: An order requiring a defendant to live up to his agreement in a contract.

Deed: A title to real property.

Defamation of Character: Injury to a plaintiff's reputation by libel or slander. See also *libel* and *slander*.

Default: The failure of a party to a legal procedure to perform an act required by law.

Defendant: The party sued in a civil suit or the accused in a criminal trial.

Demurrer: A motion for dismissal on the allegation that a plaintiff does not have proper grounds to bring suit.

Deposition: The written testimony of a witness, taken under oath elsewhere than in court.

Directory Judgment: A court order requiring a defendant to perform some act.

Disclosure Proceedings: A demand by either side in a

lawsuit that the opponent produce, before trial, all documents to be used in evidence. Also called *discovery proceedings.*

Discovery Proceedings: See *disclosure proceedings.*

Dissolution of Marriage: A decree issued in a few states which is similar to divorce but ends a marriage without attaching fault to either party.

Diversity of Citizenship Case: A legal controversy between a citizen and an alien or between residents of different states.

Divorce: A decree ending a marriage, granted to the party deemed by the court to be faultless and against the spouse judged to be at fault. See also *absolute divorce.*

Ejectment: An action to recover real property.

Encumbrance: A lien or other burden on property.

Enjoin: To order a person to perform or desist from an act.

Equity: A system of supplemental law which corrects the sometimes unfair operation of inflexible, literally applied law by permitting judges the latitude of using fairness as a guide to their decisions when rigid application of the law would result in injustice. See also *court of equity.*

Escrow: Property conditionally delivered to a third person, not the owner, who holds it until certain conditions have been met, then delivers it to the new owner.

Estate: The property of a deceased person. Also the assets of a living person.

Eviction: The ouster of a tenant from occupancy of real property.

Exception: A formal disagreement by an attorney to a ruling by the court.

Execution: Proceedings to enforce a judgment, such as a direction to a sheriff to take such steps as are necessary to collect a money judgment.

Executor or Executrix: The person designated in a will to administer the estate.

Exemption: The right of a debtor to retain certain property free from claims of creditors.

Exhibit: A document or other item tendered as evidence during trial.

Ex Parte: Literally "from a part," a term used to describe trials or hearings at which only the plaintiff presents evidence and the defendant is not present; the defendant need not even have been notified of the action.

Fellow-Servant Rule: The outmoded principle that injury caused by a fellow worker leaves no cause of action against the mutual employer.

Final Decree: A divorce decree issued at the end of an interlocutory period, permanently ending the marriage and permitting remarriage. See also *interlocutory decree.*

Findings of Fact: The court's or jury's decision as to what the circumstances of a dispute are, as opposed to conclusions of law. See also *conclusions of law.*

Garnishment: The legal seizure of a debtor's income or property to satisfy his debts.

General Verdict: A jury verdict making an overall decision on all issues.

Guardian: A person charged by law to care for a minor or an incompetent person and/or manage his property and rights. Also called a *committee.*

Habeas Corpus: Literally "you should have the body," a writ commanding a person having custody of another to produce the detained person in court for the purpose of determining the legality of the custody.

Impaneling: The listing of trial jurors by the clerk of the court.

Incompetency: The lack of legal qualifications (as with a minor) or mental ability to discharge a required duty.

Indemnity: Payment for loss or damage by prior agreement.

Infant: See *minor*.

Injunction: A writ ordering a defendant either to cease or to refrain from committing some particular act.

In Personam: Literally "against a person," meaning that a defendant against whom an in personam judgment is rendered will be held personally accountable by the court for failure to satisfy the judgment and may be held in contempt of court for such failure.

Inquisitorial System: The legal system of continental Europe, in which the opposing lawyers' ethical obligation to seek out the truth supersedes their obligations to their clients.

In Rem: Literally "against a thing," meaning that a defendant against whom an in rem judgment is rendered will not be in contempt of court for failure to satisfy the judgment but is merely liable for further civil action to collect on the part of the plaintiff.

Interlocutory Decree: A preliminary decree of divorce which requires a certain period of time to pass before a final decree is granted permitting remarriage. See also *final decree*.

Intestate: Having made no will.

Involuntary Petition of Bankruptcy: A bankruptcy proceeding initiated by creditors. See also *petition of bankruptcy*.

Judgment: The official decision of a court of justice.

Judgment Creditor: A person who has obtained a money judgment against a debtor.

Judgment Debtor: A person against whom a money judgment has been entered.

Judgment Lien: A judgment against real property.

Judgment of Foreclosure: A court order requiring the sale of real property at public auction in order to pay the liens against it.

Judicial Separation: See *decree of legal separation.*

Judiciary: The courts in general.

Jurisdiction: The limitation on the types of cases a court has authority to try. Also the geographic area over which it has authority.

Justice of the Peace: A magistrate of an inferior court with extremely limited jurisdiction.

Lease: A rental contract.

Levy: To seize and sell property to satisfy an execution.

Libel: The publication of defamatory matter in writing or printing or the representation of defamatory matter in pictures, cartoons, statues, or other media. See also *defamation of character.*

Lien: A monetary claim against an item of property, either real or personal.

Limited Divorce: See *decree of legal separation.*

Litigant: Either party to a civil suit.

Magistrate: A judge, usually of an inferior court.

Minor: A person under the age of legal competence, which in most places is now eighteen years old. Also called *infant.*

Mistrial: A judicial order ending a trial because of a procedural mistake that makes the just completion of the trial impossible.

Money Judgment: A court order declaring that a specific sum is owed a creditor by a debtor.

Mortgage: A lien against real property.

Motion: An application to the court by either side for some specific order.

Negligent Wrong: An unintentional but nevertheless actionable wrong.

Nominal Damages: A token award made when a defendant has been proved at fault, but the plaintiff has failed to establish any appreciable injury.

Notary Public: A public officer empowered to take oaths, acknowledge signatures, and authenticate documents.

Oath: A solemn attestation of the truth of testimony.

Objection: A formal complaint by one attorney against an action, statement, or question of the opposing counsel during a trial.

Order: A written direction of the court other than a judgment.

Ordinance: A local law passed by the legislative body of a governmental entity less than a state.

Oyer and Terminer Court: A court constituted to hear and determine matters, usually of a criminal nature.

Patent: (1) The exclusive right, granted by the federal government, to make, use, and sell an invention for a specified period. (2) An instrument by which the government conveys public land to an individual.

Personal Bankruptcy: Bankruptcy of an individual, as opposed to business bankruptcy.

Personal Property: All possessions other than real property.

Petition: See *complaint*.

Petition of Bankruptcy: A request to a federal district court for the court to declare a debtor bankrupt, take over control of his property, sell it off, and prorate the proceedings among his creditors. See also *invol-*

untary petition of bankruptcy and *voluntary petition of bankruptcy.*

Plaintiff: The party bringing suit in a civil case.

Plea: A formal allegation of what is claimed by one side or denied by the other in a civil suit. Also a declaration of guilt, nonguilt, or no contest in a criminal trial.

Pledge: The transfer of possession of, or title to, personal property as security for a debt.

Power of Attorney: Written authorization to another to act as one's agent.

Prima-Facie Evidence: Literally "at first sight," evidence strong enough to support the claim of one side in the absence of counter evidence.

Privity: A direct mutual relationship between the two or more parties to a transaction.

Probate: The branch of law concerned with estates and wills. See also *surrogate* and *surrogate's court.*

Proceeding for an Accounting: See *action for an accounting.*

Punitive Damages: A monetary award in addition to compensatory damages when it has been shown that an injury was maliciously inflicted. See also *compensatory damages.*

Real Property: Land and things attached to the land, such as buildings or other structures.

Receiver: A person appointed by the court to receive and preserve property pending the outcome of a legal procedure.

Receivership: Supervision of a business in financial trouble by a court and its management by a court-appointed receiver.

Referee: A person to whom a court refers certain legal proceedings and who has limited power to act in the court's name.

Remand: To send back a case from an appellate court to a lower court for corrective action. Also to return a defendant to custody.

Remedy: The redressing of an injury or the enforcement of a right.

Replevin: An action to recover personal property unlawfully taken or held.

Replication: A plaintiff's second submission to the court, following his initial complaint and the defendant's answer, disputing the arguments in the answer and answering any counterclaim. Also called a *reply*. See also *complaint* and *answer*.

Reply: See *replication*.

Respondent: The party who answers a petition in a court proceeding. Also the party against whom an appeal is taken.

Restraining Order: A court order enjoining a party to suspend a practice objected to by a plaintiff until the court can hold a hearing on whether or not an injunction should be issued. Also called a *temporary restraining order*.

Restraint of Trade: Illegal activity designed to eliminate business competition.

Satisfaction: A document acknowledging satisfaction of a money judgment, furnished by a plaintiff to the defendant upon payment of the judgment.

Security Agreement: See *chattel mortgage*.

Separate Maintenance: See *decree of legal separation*.

Separation Agreement: A voluntary arrangement, with court permission, under which married persons may legally live apart.

Sequestration: A court order to a sheriff or other officer of the court to hold the property under dispute until a decision is handed down.

Service of Process: The delivery of a summons, a subpoena, or a notification of an action against the person served.

Slander: Defamation by spoken words or gestures. See also *defamation of character*.

Special Verdict: A jury decision on some specific question of fact whose answer is necessary before the judge can rule on a matter of law.

Statement: See *complaint*.

Statute: An act of Congress or of a state legislature.

Statute of Limitations: The law fixing the maximum time after an alleged injury in which a civil action must be started or the maximum time after an alleged crime in which a criminal charge must be brought against the accused.

Stipulation: An agreement as to certain mutually accepted facts between opposing attorneys.

Subpoena: A writ commanding a witness to appear in court to give testimony.

Substantive Law: Law that regulates legal rights.

Summary Judgment: A decision handed down by the court at any point of a civil trial, based on the evidence so far submitted, when the court feels the evidence has been sufficient to make a judgment without taking time to hear any more.

Summons: A notice to a defendant in a civil suit that an action has been commenced against him, and he must appear to answer it within a stated time.

Surrogate: In some states the judge of the court responsible for probate. See also *probate*.

Surrogate's Court: The term used for probate court in some states. See also *probate*.

Temporary Restraining Order: See *restraining order*.

Testament: That part of a will disposing of personal property.

Title: The evidence of a person's ownership of property.

Tort: A civil wrong committed upon the person or property of another, other than a breach of contract, which constitutes grounds for seeking damages.

Trial: The judicial examination of a legal controversy.

Trial by Battle: A primitive method of settling civil disputes, revived during the Middle Ages, in which a ritualized duel, seldom fought to death, determined which party was in the right.

Trial by Ordeal: The barbaric custom of deciding guilt or innocence, or sometimes civil litigations, by submitting a defendant to some physical test, such as immersing him in water to see whether he drowned or not.

Trust: The holding of property by one person for the benefit of another.

Trustee: One who administers a trust.

Unsecured Loan: A loan granted on signature only, with nothing put up as security by the borrower.

Venue: The place designated for trial.

Voluntary Petition of Bankruptcy: A bankruptcy proceeding initiated by the debtor himself. See also *petition of bankruptcy.*

Waiver: A relinquishing of rights.

Ward: A minor or an incompetent person under guardianship.

Warrant: A document directing a public officer to make an arrest or a search or to perform certain other acts.

Witness: A person who observes a transaction or the signing of a signature on a legal document. Also a person who testifies in court.

Workmen's Compensation: An insurance program, with premiums paid by employers, to compensate employees for injuries sustained in the course of their employment, without requiring proof of negligence on the part of employers.

Writ: A court order directed to a public officer, such as a sheriff or a district attorney, or to a private individual, requiring the performance of a certain act.

Writ of Mandamus: An order to force a public official to perform a mandatory duty he has failed to perform or to force a company or a corporation official to perform some act required either by statute or by company bylaws that he has failed to perform.

INDEX

www.ingramcontent.com/pod-product-compliance
Lightning Source LLC
Chambersburg PA
CBHW020201200326
41521CB00005BA/212